THE STORY OF

The Oaks And Oaks Park

BY
MARGARET
CUNNINGHAM

Sutton Leisure

Sutton Leisure Services
The Old Court House, Throwley Way, Sutton SM1 4AF

ISBN 0 907335 27 6

© Text: Margaret Cunningham
Design: The Studio 081 770 4605

Printed by DASPRINT Limited
53 Lydden Grove, London SW18 4LW

The London Borough of Sutton wishes to thank
The Oaks Sports Centre, Geoff Horley and Margaret Cunningha
for their sponsorship in the production of this book.

CONTENTS

		Page
Acknowledgements		i
Illustrations acknowledgements		i
Introduction		iii
Chapter 1.	In the Beginning	1
Chapter 2.	Lambert's Oaks	4
Chapter 3.	John Burgoyne and the Stanley Family	11
Chapter 4.	A Famous Fête and a Reluctant Bride	20
Chapter 5.	An Unfinished Castle, a Cricket Match and a Defeated General	32
Chapter 6.	New Sporting Events and some Theatrical Pursuits	39
Chapter 7.	The Idyllic Years	45
Chapter 8.	A Desirable Country Residence	53
Chapter 9.	Under Public Ownership	64
Chapter 10.	The End of The Oaks	68
Chapter 11.	The Oaks Park and Sports Centre	80
Appendix I.	The Oaks Mansion and its Estate in 1912	89
Appendix II.	Yardages of Proposed pre-1939 Golf Course	98
References		99

ACKNOWLEDGEMENTS

My sincere and grateful thanks are given to everyone who helped during my research work on the book, especially to Miss Mary Batchelor; to Miss June Broughton for her invaluable assistance in obtaining information from Sutton Central Library's local history collection and archives as well as elsewhere, and for her editorial work; to Miss Heather Cant; to Mr. Doug Cluett for his advice and editorial assistance; to Miss Ruth Goodchild of Banstead and Reigate Library Services at Banstead Library; to the late Mrs. H. Herbecq; to Mr. Geoff Horley and Mr. E.F. Bennett of Alpha Green Limited; to Mrs. Hilary Horley; to Miss Alison Kearns lately the Archivist at Sutton Central Library; to Mr. Tim Neligan of United Racecourses Limited; to Mr. Brian Pote-Hunt for organising the publication of the book; to Mr. Stan Pullen; to Mr. Gordon Rookledge; to Mr. Joe Rowe for his artwork and preparation of the book for printing; to Mr. Len Sandell for supplying me with copies of the Carshalton Urban District Council's Minute Books; to Mr. Andrew Skelton for his critisms and help; to Professor Michael Wilks for his helpful criticisms of my first draft copy of the book; to the staff at the Surrey Record Office, Kingston-upon-Thames; to members of the staff on Level 4 of the Central Library, Sutton, and in the late Reference Library at Wallington.

As every effort has been made to prevent me making errors, any that have been left in the book are my responsibility.

ILLUSTRATIONS ACKNOWLEDGEMENTS

Copies of most of the illustrations are to be found in the Local Studies Collection of the Heritage Division, Sutton Leisure Services. Thanks are due to the following for permission to reproduce their photographs: Marylebone Cricket Club; The Frick Collection, New York; Sport & General Press Agency; The Royal Commission on the Historical Monuments of England; and Mrs. A. Maynard-Taylor.

INTRODUCTION

Today, not many people who visit the Oaks Park remember the old mansion after which it is named. Even fewer visitors realise its importance in our local and national history, and its connection with two of the most famous events in the annual horse-racing calendar - the Oaks and the Derby.

The story of the lands which became the Oaks Park began in prehistoric times, and the history of the house commenced in the fourteenth century. All of the owners and occupiers from the late thirteenth century onwards have contributed to the story of The Oaks and its estate.

Members of the royal family and the nobility were entertained at The Oaks in the late eighteenth and early nineteenth centuries. In the reign of George III, the lawns were the scene of the most famous party given at that time - the Fête Champêtre - held in honour of the forthcoming marriage of Lord Edward Stanley, who became the twelfth Earl of Derby, and Lady Betty Hamilton. A temporary pavilion designed for this event by the famous architect, Robert Adam, was erected on the lawn near the house, and provided a ballroom, tea and supper rooms for the guests.

King George III and Queen Charlotte visited The Oaks, and so did their son, the Prince of Wales, who became the Prince Regent. The elite of Georgian and Regency society, including those in the sporting world and members of successive governments, were among the visitors here, especially during the annual horse-racing events on the adjoining downlands, and on Epsom Downs.

The house was called Lambert's Oaks until the late eighteenth century, when it became known as The Oaks, and additions were made to it in the neo-Gothic castle style. The work was not completed, and, although further alterations were carried out on it after a fire in the mid-nineteenth century, this unusual house remained outwardly unchanged despite some damage to it in World War II, until, due to neglect, it was demolished between December 1956, and November 1959. The last turret was pulled down at the beginning of 1960.

In the past, some misinformation has been written about The Oaks, its tenants and owners. I have endeavoured to present its story as accurately as possible, so that before its importance in our local heritage fades completely from living memory it can be restored - if only on paper.

Margaret Cunningham, October 1993.

Chapter 1   IN THE BEGINNING

The first traces of man on lands which became today's Oaks Park, the golf courses, and the Oaks Farm, began in prehistoric times. Evidence that Stone Age man came here was provided by some undated flints, possibly Neolithic (late Stone Age from c.3200 B.C.) which were uncovered in 1968, during the fieldwork carried out in preparation for laying a section of a large gas pipeline (the outer London ring main) through the Park, from Little Woodcote to Woodmansterne. The pipe was laid along the northern edge of two of the present-day golf course fairways (the second of the nine-hole, and sixteenth of the eighteen-hole courses) before going through the woodlands, then across Croydon Lane and on to the Oaks farmlands. During the pipe-laying operations more worked flints were found, including one which was described as 'a true pygmy' (i.e. a microlith) and part of a large coarse core. [1,2] Microliths are small flints dating from the Mesolothic (Middle Stone Age from c.1200-3000 B.C.).

The disturbance of the soil in excavations for the pipeline through ploughland by the outbuildings of the Oaks Farm probably led to the discovery of a good example of a Neolithic discoidal (circular) knife. In size, it measured seventy-five by sixty-seven millimetres, with only minor damage in several places, and its edge was ground and polished all the way round. [1]

The first people known to have lived in the area established an enclosed settlement on top of the hill opposite the eastern side of the Oaks Park. The site of their village, or hillfort, is situated at the southern end of the grounds of Queen Mary's Hospital, and adjoins the present-day smallholdings. It was occupied, possibly not continuously, from the Late Bronze Age (1000 B.C. - 700 B.C.) until the Late Iron Age (700 B.C. - 43 A.D.) [3] and was a probable regional focus, with control over a tract of downland about ten kilometres across. [4] Its proximity to the Park, golf courses, and the Oaks Farm, suggests that these lands were included in the pattern of farming which usually surrounded such early villages, and were used for grazing sheep, cattle, and for growing grain.

Three burial mounds, or barrows, stood on the north-western side of the enclosed settlement, and to the north of the Oaks Park. These could have been of Bronze Age origins, or earlier; [5] but, because of their destruction over two centuries by constant ploughing of the land on which they stood, it has not been possible accurately to assess their original date. They had been left untouched in the seventeenth and early eighteenth centuries. William Camden mentioned them in his *Britannia* of 1586; and, in his *Antiquities of Surrey* (1736) Nathaniel Salmon called them "Gally Hills" , or "Devil's Mounds", suggesting that some kind of local folklore about them was circulating then. ('Gally' is an obsolete word meaning to frighten or scare). Later, they provided the name of "Barrow Hedges" for the house which had been built near them by the end of the seventeenth century. [5]

To date, no artefacts of Roman origin have been recorded from the Oaks Park or farmlands. The earliest pottery discovered in "operation pipeline" through the parklands was some coarse, eighteenth century sherds at the northern end of the park, and, in the trench near the site of the old mansion, a collection of mid-eighteenth century glazed sherds was found. [2] There was some form of Roman habitation in the area. A Roman lamp was unearthed in a garden in Pine Walk (seen by the author, but its present whereabouts unknown); and a silver spoon was dug up in Barrow Hedges; as well as a horse skeleton and pottery in The Gallop on Carshalton Downs. Pottery and coins have been found during excavations on the site of the enclosure in Queen Mary's Hospital grounds. [6]

Not far from the eastern edge of the modern parklands, and somewhere in the old Woodcote Warren (which included part of Little Woodcote) was the alleged site of a Roman town, or city. In the seventeenth century, John Evelyn wrote to John Aubrey about Woodcote and said,quoting Burton's *Notes upon Antoninus's Itinerary:* "Roman Coins, Urns and Bricks, and co." were dug up by "the Rusticks", and traces of buildings could be seen, also many old wells. [7] All of these gave rise to much speculation by learned gentlemen in the seventeenth and eighteenth centuries as to whether it was the site of the city called Noiomagus by Ptolemy, and Noviomagus by Antoninus. (The Antonine Itinerary was the Roman equivalent to the modern A.A. Guide.)

Evidence of Saxon occupation near the Oaks Park has been found in the grounds of Queen Mary's Hospital, where the discovery of some burial urns indicated the possibility of a Saxon cemetery here, and probable use of the site of the prehistoric enclosure by the Saxons. [3] They gave the name of Odermerestor to their settlement about a mile away to the south of the present-day parklands; "ode" being derived from the Anglo-Saxon "wode" - a wood; "mere" - a lake; and "tor" - a high point. In the years before the Norman conquest, the Saxon lord, Azor, held Odermerestor in the reign of Edward the Confessor (1042-1066) as well as nearby Beddintone (Beddington). [8]

After the arrival of the Normans in 1066, and the establishment of their manorial system, the lands comprised of the modern Oaks Park, golf courses, and the Oaks Farm, became part of Woodmansterne, and remained in its jurisdiction until changes were made to the parish boundaries with the creation of the Rural and Urban District Councils at the end of the nineteenth century when they became part of Carshalton Urban District. [5] When William of Normandy came to England, he was accompanied by, among others, Baldwin, Lord of le Sap, and Radulphus de Lambert. It has been alleged that the Lamberts held land in Woodmansterne from the time of the conquest, but this is not true. [9] The tenant-in-chief when the Domesday Survey was made in 1086 was one of Baldwin's three sons, Richard de Bienfaite (who became known as Richard of Tonbridge, or Clare). He also held Azor's manor at Beddington. [10]

The Domesday Survey showed that the manor of Woodmansterne contained fifteen hides but paid no tax. (In those days, about one hundred to one hundred and twenty acres were called a hide, and a carucate was a measure of land which was as much as could be tilled with one plough in a year.) There were three carucates of arable land, and two carucates in demesne (the estate of the manor house). The inhabitants included a villein (a feudal serf) and twelve cottars with three carucates (a cottar was a peasant who paid rent in the form of labour for his cottage). Altogether there were eighteen villeins living in Woodmansterne. There was a church, and one mill to the value of 20s. and about four acres of meadow. The wood "yields 10 Hogs" meaning that payment in kind was made to the lord of the manor for the right to use the woods or pasture for swine. [8, 11]

Woodmansterne's Saxon name of Odermerestor lasted through the eleventh century until it became Wudemareschorn in the twelfth, then Wudmannesthorne in the thirteenth, and Wodemansterne or Wodemansthorne in the fourteenth century. Although the manor was held by the descendants of Richard of Tonbridge, as overlords, at some early date part of the lands were subinfeudated [10] (granted in fee) to the tenants there, with the exception of the downlands of the modern Oaks Park and farm. These passed into the ownership of the Pembroke branch of the family, and, through lack of a male heir, by marriage of a co-heiress, Isabel, to William Marshall; only to return again to the Clare family, when Gilbert de Clare married his cousin, Isabel, one of Marshall's daughters, who was a co-heiress to her father's estates, which included those in Woodmansterne. [9] In 1218, Gilbert obtained the earldom of Gloucester, with its great territorial Honour (a group of manors administered as a unit). [12]

Before his death in Brittany in 1230, [12] in the reign of Henry III, Gilbert granted part of his estate in Woodmansterne to John Lambert, who was one of the descendants of Radulphus de Lambert. John held these lands freely of the Honour of Gloucester, and paid no tax or service for them. Also, he had other estates in Surrey, and was a Citizen of London. John's property in Woodmansterne remained in the possession of his descendants, and their relatives, for over another five centuries. [9] It has been alleged that, after a grove of oak trees had been planted by them, they built a house here. Their estate became known as Lambert's Oaks, and this part of the Lambert family was called the Lamberts of Woodmansterne. [13]

Chapter 2   LAMBERT'S OAKS

There is no information regarding the date of the first house in this part of Woodmansterne. It has been claimed that Lambert's Oaks was the seat of the Lambert family in the parish from the latter half of the thirteenth century until about 1660. [14] Possibly, a mediaeval building stood on the site of the outbuildings belonging to the old Oaks mansion, but no evidence has been found to substantiate its exact position. [15] The downlands around the Lamberts' estate were mostly used for sheep-farming at that time, and the parish was described as 'mainly sheepwalks'. [10]

In 1301, John Lambert's son, John, was the first member of his family to use the title "of Woodmansterne", which suggests that he had built a house at Lambert's Oaks by then. He conveyed the property in 1333 to his son, another John, who also owned lands in Guildford and "elsewhere". When this John died, the estate passed to his third boy, Radulphus, who was alive in 1377, and then it was left to Radulphus's second son, John Lambert of Banstead and Woodmansterne. After the latter's death, it was owned by his heir, another John, who bought more properties in Banstead from John de Bures in 1432. The next owner was John's eldest son, yet another John, who, in turn, bequeathed it to his third son, also called John! [9] It seems likely that this was the John Lambert who had a stone slab inscribed with his name, and the date 1501, and placed it beneath one of the beech trees which grew here in the grounds of Lambert's Oaks. [8]

John enlarged his estate in 1513, when he bought Shortes Place in Woodmansterne from a John Cotes. This house was situated in a small park opposite the church. [9] Early in the fourteenth century, Adam a Lye had held land here called "Shortesland" which he conveyed to Henry and Robert de la Cocharde. The next owner was Reginald le Forester, who was an important local landowner in Beddington and Bandon in the reign of Edward III, and became Sheriff of Surrey in 1334, and a Member of Parliament for the county in 1348. [8] He sold the house to Adam de St. Alban, and, in 1370, it was purchased from his son, John, by Robert Cocces, or Cotes, whose family held it until John Lambert acquired it in 1513. [10] The Lamberts then kept it in their possession for over another three hundred years. [9]

In 1515, John Lambert purchased Perrotts Manor in Banstead, and held lands in Coulsdon, Chipstead, Horne, Horley and "other places". He married Joan Wellys, or Waleys, of Woodmansterne, and they had six children. Later, John's eldest son, Jeffrey, lived at Shortes Place, and already owned properties in Chipstead, Coulsdon, Clandon and Gatton, when he inherited Lambert's Oaks on his father's death. He married five times, and his wives presented him with a total of nineteen children. [9] In 1537, he bought Garratts Hall in Banstead, [8] and some of his descendants lived here until 1708. When he died in about 1566/1567, he left Lambert's Oaks and Shortes Place to one of his sons, Roger. In the same year, a distant connection by marriage was made with another locally famous family, the Carews of Beddington, when Roger's brother, Nicholas, married Ann Moys, who was a great granddaughter of the late Sir Richard Carew. [9]

Roger Lambert moved from Lambert's Oaks in 1584, and went to live at Shortes Place. Some fine Tudor panelling was installed in this house, as well as a carved mantelpiece with Roger's coat of arms on it, together with his initials and those of his wife, Elizabeth. He joined the Earl of Leicester's army in 1585, and went to fight the Spanish invaders of the Low Countries in support of William of Orange. On his return to England, he brought back some fire-dogs of Dutch origin for his home in the village of Woodmansterne. [9]

The eldest of Roger and Elizabeth's three sons, Daniel, married in 1592, when he was twenty-one years old. His bride was Susan, the daughter of William Wonham of Wonham Manor in Betchworth, Surrey. They had six children, and their first child, another Roger, was born in 1601. Daniel inherited his father's properties, including Lambert's Oaks, in 1617, but did not live for many years afterwards. He died in 1622 and his Woodmansterne estates passed to his young son, Roger. [9]

During the sixteenth century, the large tract of downs around Lambert's Oaks had become a very popular area for hunting and horse-racing. [9] These downlands then stretched westwards from Croydon, above the villages of Beddington, Carshalton, Sutton, Cheam, Ewell and Epsom, and as far south as Reigate, and included Banstead Downs. There was a good variety of game to hunt here, including plenty of conies (rabbits), foxes, hares, badgers, partridges, pheasants, and "all kinds of vermin", to provide the field-sports, which not only attracted the attention of royalty, [17] but also had an important influence on the   history of The Oaks.

Hunting was the favourite sport of Henry VIII, [17] and there can be little doubt that it was part of the entertainments offered to him on his visits to his great friend and favourite, Sir Nicholas Carew at Beddington. Their friendship began in their childhood spent together at the royal court, where Sir Nicholas's father, Sir Richard Carew, spent a good deal of his time in the service of Henry VII, and it ended with Sir Nicholas's death on the scaffold on 3rd March, 1539, after being charged with treason. There was a tradition that this was as a result of a foolish quarrel with the King, allegedly over a game of bowls. The real reasons probably had more to do with court intrigue and Henry's desire for estates made up of lands inherited from Sir Richard, as well as manors in Banstead, Walton on the Hill, Epsom and Sutton, previously given as rewards for loyalty to His Majesty. [18, 19]. These were added to the King's newly-acquired Nonsuch estate on the site of the village of Cuddington adjoining Banstead Downs (owned by the King) and provided vast hunting grounds for the King's pleasure. Ironically, Henry died in 1547, before his palace at Nonsuch was completed, though it was so in its essential features, and he had stayed there after it became habitable. [17]

The Carews' local estates, including the downlands at Woodcote on the eastern side of Lambert's Oaks, were regained by Sir Nicholas's only son and heir, Francis, in 1554, in the reign of Mary I. Subsequently, he was knighted by Elizabeth I in 1576, [18] and the Queen visited his home, the manor house at Beddington, on a number of occasions. [18, 20] Her Majesty had inherited her father's love of hunting and horse-racing, and was a frequent visitor to Nonsuch Palace. [17] She also stayed at the Archbishop of Canterbury's palace in Croydon between 1559 and 1575, and 1585 and 1587, so that she could take part in hunting on the downs, and watch the annual horse-races held there around each May Day. [20] Her successor, James I, gave Nonsuch to his Queen, Anne of Denmark, in 1603. During the early years of his reign (1603-1625) the King and his two sons, the Princes Henry and Charles, enjoyed hawking and hunting on the downlands during their visits to the Palace. [17]

By this time, horse-racing was well-established on the downlands around Lambert's Oaks. It is thought that, in 1625, a four-mile course ran across the downs from the north-east to a point on the present-day one at Epsom Downs, [21] and these races continued to be popular in Charles I's reign (1625-1649). After 1632, the popularity of the nearby village of Epsom increased with the discovery of a medicinal spring and its benefits, and it quickly grew into a spa town which, for a while, was more popular than Tunbridge Wells. The races were held then on the adjacent downs daily at noon, as part of the entertainments offered to the visitors. [22]

It seems likely that some race meetings were held throughout the Civil War. In 1648, the Earl of Clarendon recorded that a party of Royalists met on the downs under the pretence of a horse-race, but, in reality, the purpose of the meeting was to cause a diversion on the King's behalf. [23] The affair ended in a fierce battle with the Parliamentary forces, and great losses were sustained on both sides.

Racing ceased under the Commonwealth rule, but commenced again after the restoration of the monarchy in 1660. Charles II was present at the first race-meeting, which took place at Epsom on 7th March, 1661. [23] Throughout his reign, the King spent much of his time here racing, hawking and hunting. He built his hunting box, The Warren, on the downlands above the town of Epsom.[22]

The seventeenth-century writer, Richard Blome, said that the Banstead Downs "affordeth great delight for Hawking, Hunting and Horse-races." The famous diarist, Samuel Pepys, was another racing enthusiast. He intended to visit the downs on 25th May, 1663, to see a "famous race", but heard in time that it had been cancelled "because the Lords do sit in Parliament today". Two days later, he recorded in his diary that he regretted being unable to join "the great throng" to Banstead Downs where a "great horse-race and foot-race" were held. [22]

The most common form of competition at these race-meetings was a "match" in which two horses would run over an agreed course, with the owners putting up the stakes. In the alternative type of race, the prize was a silver cup, or bell, subscribed for by local

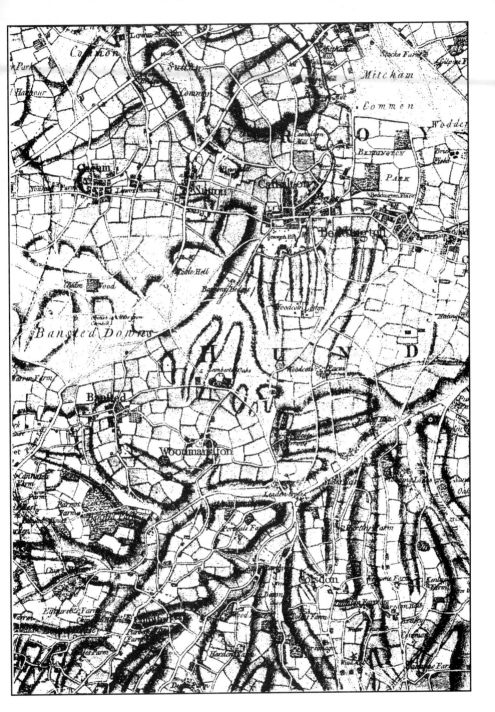

Part of John Rocque's map of Surrey in 1762 showing Lambert's Oaks in the centre.

"worthies", and these races were run in the form of heats, often over very long courses. The horse that won the first two heats was the outright winner, so that, usually, it was the strongest, not the fastest, animal which won the prize. Plates (prizes) and weight limits had been the only refinements to this sport introduced by the end of the seventeenth century. [24]

In January, 1695, an announcement appeared in the *London Gazette* about two "Plates run for yearly, three times successively, each Plate to be £20 price. The first to be run 14th February next, and all the others on May-Day and Bartholomew Day in every year, till three years are expired." The rules were that any of the horses entered for the Plate must be "at any of the Contributors' Stables in Carshalton, Barrowhedges, or elsewhere, fourteen days before. The weight ten stone." The stake of three guineas for each horse had to be paid to the Clerk of the Course seven days before the "Plate Day", otherwise a payment of five guineas could be made at any time. [24]

Barrow Hedges, which was situated on the north side of Lambert's Oaks in a small valley towards Carshalton village, was also a place of some importance in the history of racing on the local downlands. It was mentioned again in the same newspaper in 1698, when an announcement was made that the horses running in the Banstead Downs Plate could be inspected here, or at one of the contributors' stables. In the early part of the eighteenth century, advertisements began to appear in the London newspapers for the Greyhound Inn at Carshalton, which was described as another place where race-horses entered for the races on the downlands were available for inspection, and that the Inn was a venue for cock-fighting. [5]

It is not known when the first house at Barrow Hedges was built, but there was some kind of establishment here at the end of the seventeenth century and beginning of the eighteenth, when it was owned by the Short family of Carshalton. In 1712, it became the property of Sir William Scawen, who acquired it from Joseph, George, Peter, Elizabeth and Susannah Short, and it was included in their half of the Manor of Carshalton, which they sold to Sir William, and contained a total of four messuages, four cottages, four gardens, three hundred acres of land, fifty acres of meadow, one hundred acres of pasture and fifty acres of "furze and heath". [25] Sir William was a Director of the Bank of England between 1699 and 1722 (with statutory intervals). [26] He came to Carshalton in 1696, after buying a moiety of the manor, including the house in Carshalton Park where he lived. [27] He died in October, 1722, and left his estates to his nephew, Thomas Scawen, [28] and Barrow Hedges remained in his family's possession until 1779, during which time it was occupied by tenants. [5]

Horse-racing on the downlands around Lambert's Oaks and Barrow Hedges, and above Epsom, attracted Queen Anne's consort, Prince George of Denmark, who loved this sport. [29] In 1711, John Toland, the theologian and author, described the Epsom scene in a long letter to his lady-friend, Eudoxa. In his description of the downs, he wrote: " The great number of Gentlemen and Ladies, that take the air every evening and morning on horseback, and that range either singly, or in separate companies, over every hill and dale, is a most entertaining object. You can never miss of it on the fine grounds of the new orbicular Race, which may well be termed a rural Cirque." He also mentioned: "The four mile course over the Warrenhouse to Carshalton, a village abounding in delicious springs ...".[30]

Although Epsom's popularity as a spa began to decline after 1715, racing on the Downs continued to prosper in Georgian times, and regular spring and summer meetings had been established by 1730.[22, 29] In the early eighteenth century, the races on Banstead Downs were described by a German visitor to England, Conrad von Uffenbach, who seemed astonished by the proceedings when he rode there one afternoon at three o'clock. He saw "vast crowds on horseback, both men and females, many of the latter wore men's clothes and feathered hats ...", which, he observed, " is quite usual in England". He was amazed to find that the racecourse was "so uneven and hilly". It was marked out with coloured stakes, or posts, "round which the horses had to run twice in one race", and the last post had a flag stuck in it. He saw the hut where the horses were taken and rubbed down after the races, which began and ended near it.[24] This hut could have been the "Rubing house" at Barrow Hedges shown on the map of Surrey made by John Senex in 1729. Herr von Uffenbach asked his servant to time one of the four-mile heats, and was impressed to learn that it took nine minutes. He also commented on the behaviour of the noisy crowd, who galloped about on horseback during the races, "one rushing here, and the other there". If any of these riders got in the way of a horse taking part in the race, they were attacked by the people who had backed it![24]

Meanwhile, changes had taken place at Lambert's Oaks. Roger Lambert had become impoverished due to the Commonwealth rule, when high taxation was imposed as a penalty on landowners who had supported the royalist cause. Roger managed to hold on to his properties until his death in 1668, but when these passed to his son, another Roger, he sold Lambert's Oaks and Shortes Place to his relative, Jeffrey Lambert of Borough (Burgh) in Banstead.[9]

Jeffrey's eldest son, John, was eighteen years old when he inherited his father's properties in 1681. He lived at Shortes Place, and although Lambert's Oaks remained in his possession and that of his descendants until 1788, it was no longer used by the Lambert family. Instead, it was leased to a succession of tenants, who were attracted to the house by the many sporting activities on the surrounding downlands.[9]

As yet, it has not been possible to discover the exact date when Lambert's Oaks was leased to its first tenants, who were a group of gentlemen known as the "Hunters' Club".[13] It seems likely that they took out a lease on the property at some time after 1668. The history of the house between then and 1756 remains unclear, and various conjectures have been made about it.

It has been alleged that Lambert's Oaks was built by the Hunters' Club as a place of festivity during the hunting seasons, also that it was an ale-house. [13] Probably, the sporting gentlemen enlarged what had, previously, been a smaller house, which has been described by a member of the Lambert family as the seat of the Lamberts in the parish of Woodmansterne from the latter half of the thirteenth century until c. 1660. There can be little doubt that quantities of ale and other drinks were imbibed here by the members of the Hunters' Club, but a small ale-house called "The Lambert's Oaks" stood between the house and Woodmansterne Church up until c.1800, when it was pulled down, leaving the village without a public-house for almost another hundred years. [14]

The owner of Lambert's Oaks, John Lambert, died in 1721, and the house passed to his eldest son, Jeffrey, who lived at Shortes Place until his death in 1742, when his son and heir, John, inherited both houses. The properties remained in his possession until he died in 1771, and left them to his only surviving son, William, who was a minor aged ten. [9] During this period, a Mr Simmons had taken over the lease of Lambert's Oaks, allegedly after the Hunters' Club left there, [13] probably in the early part of the eighteenth century.

The next alleged tenant was Sir Thomas Gosling, the banker, [13] and it has been conjectured that he employed the architect, Sir Robert Taylor, to rebuild the house. Its design was common to all other villas designed by Sir Robert, i.e. a five-bay elevation, a hipped roof in place of a central pediment, lower flanking bays and elongated mutules (prominent beam ends) at eaves level, as shown by a reconstruction of the house from Robert Adam's plans c 1774, and by an engraved view of it in 1819.[31] Thus, this conjecture would date Sir Thomas's tenancy to include the years 1753 to 1756. Sir Robert Taylor's career as an architect began in about 1753, whereas, previously, he had been a sculptor, and his works included the figure of Britannia in the centre of the principal facade of the Bank of England, and sculpture in the pediment of the Mansion House. His patrons for his architectural designs included those in banking and in the city. [32]

In his description of Lambert's Oaks, Mr F.A.H. Lambert did not mention either Mr Simmons, or Sir Thomas Gosling, as tenants of the property, but stated that it had been let to the Hunters' Club. [9] Therefore, it is possible that these two gentlemen were members of the Club, and, successively, were in charge of it. Also, if the conjecture is true that Sir Thomas employed Sir Robert Taylor to rebuild the house, this would account for the statement made in another source that the Hunters' Club built it. However, all sources of information agree that the next tenant here was John Burgoyne, who took out a lease for a period of ninety-nine years, and came to the downlands to "hunt and shoot".

Chapter 3
JOHN BURGOYNE AND THE STANLEY FAMILY

By the time John Burgoyne took out his lease on Lambert's Oaks, he had married into one of the most important noble families of England, and was the son-in-law of Lord Edward Stanley, the eleventh Earl of Derby. The Earl had inherited his title and large estate in 1736, from his distant relative, Lord James, the tenth Earl, who died without any male heirs to inherit the entailed properties. [33]

John Burgoyne was born on 4th February, 1722, at the Burgoyne's family home of Sutton Park in Bedfordshire, and was the second son of Captain John Burgoyne and a grandson of Sir John Burgoyne, third Baronet. He was educated at Westminster School, where he became a close friend of the eleventh Earl of Derby's eldest boy, James Stanley, Lord Strange (a title inherited by the second Earl through his mother, and passed down to each successive heir to the earldom). [32, 34] Their friendship lasted throughout Lord Strange's lifetime, and had many beneficial effects on John's life.

As a second son, John had little money of his own, and he entered the army at an early age. In 1740, when he was eighteen years old, he became a cornet in the thirteenth Light Dragoons, and purchased a lieutenancy in the following year. While his regiment was stationed at Preston in Lancashire, he frequently visited his friend, Lord Strange, at the Stanley's family seat of Knowsley, where he met, and fell in love with, Lord Strange's younger sister, Lady Charlotte Stanley. [32, 34] Their attraction to each other did not meet with Lord Derby's approval.

Eventually, the young lovers eloped in 1743, [35] with the approval of Lord Strange. Lord Derby was so angry that he declared he would never see his daughter again, and gave her only a small sum of money on her marriage - which the bridegroom used to buy himself a captaincy in his regiment. [32] Despite its clandestine beginnings, their marriage lasted for over thirty-three years, during which time they had one daughter. [34]

Between 1743 and 1746, John and Lady Charlotte spent a very pleasant life in London, while Lord Derby was dealing with the Jacobite invasion of Lancashire. [33] In 1746, John's long-established love of gambling began to have disastrous results. His lack of funds resulted in many debts, so that, eventually, he was forced to sell his commission to pay off some of the money he and his wife owed, as well as to finance their flight to France to avoid their other creditors. [33, 34] They lived in a little cottage in Chanteloup during their seven years of exile. John studied both the French language and its literature, and obtained a good knowledge of European politics and the condition of the armies there. [32]

Fireplace in the dining-room of The Oaks. Design attributed to Sir Robert Taylor, the architect employed by John Burgoyne in 1770. RCHME Crown Copyright.

During the period of John's exile in France, his brother-in-law, Lord Strange, married Lucy, the daughter and heiress of Hugh Smith of Weald Hall in Essex, and then took the name of Smith to add before his own surname of Stanley. Their eldest child, Lord Edward Smith Stanley, was born on 12th September 1752, at their home, Patten House in Preston, Lancashire. Lord Strange's marriage to the wealthy Lucy improved his financial status, and he was able to indulge even more in his love of horse-racing and cock-fighting. He kept race-horses and fighting-cocks, and patronised the horse-races on Preston Moor, as well as regularly attending the local cock-fights there. Also, he became a member of the Jockey Club in 1754, two years after it was formed. Unfortunately, his wife, Lucy, died in 1759, but not before she had assisted her husband to make his family a very popular one in Preston, and had presented him with five children - two sons and three daughters. [32, 34, 36]

Eventually, John Burgoyne was reconciled with his father-in-law, and returned to England after Lord Derby had paid off his debts. [36] In 1756, he was able to resume his army career through the Earl's influence, and he became a Captain in the eleventh Dragoons. [32] It seems likely that he also took out his lease on Lambert's Oaks in the same year, so that he could join in the hunting activities on the adjoining downlands. It is alleged that he fitted up the house as his country residence. [37] The famous cartographer, Rocque, surveyed the counties between 1752 and 1762 before his death in the latter year. In posthumous publications of his maps of Surrey in 1762 and 1768, he showed a formal design for the grounds around Lambert's Oaks, and in the walled garden on the west of it. The Oaks Farm on the opposite side of the lane was not shown on either of the Rocque's maps, and, therefore, must have been built sometime later, perhaps in Burgoyne's "fitting up" operations, because it appeared on Lindley and Crosley's map of 1793. [38]

Undoubtedly, Lord Derby was attracted to Lambert's Oaks because of the horse-races on the adjoining downs. The Earl was equally as keen on horse-racing as his relative, James, the tenth Earl of Derby, had been. He had inherited Lord James's hunting and racing stables at Knowsley, and the race-course in Knowsley Park. From 1757 onwards, Lord Strange took over his father's duties of Lord-Lieutenant of Lancashire, and was made Chancellor of the Duchy as well as one of George III's Privy Councillors. [33] Thus, Lord Derby had more time to spare for his sporting activities, and, although John Burgoyne retained his lease on Lambert's Oaks until 1771, allegedly the Earl became his under-tenant of the house from 1759, [9] and his parties here were famous. [39] He was joined in the neighbourhood by the Duke of Devonshire, who was the rated occupier of Barrow Hedges between 1760 and 1763, [5] and, probably, used it as a place in which to entertain his friends during the hunting and racing seasons. Meanwhile, John's increasing involvement in his army career, and his entry into politics, possibly, left him with less spare time in which to visit Lambert's Oaks. He and Lady Charlotte had their home at Walton-le-Dale near Preston. [33]

At the beginning of the Seven Years' War with France in 1756, John served under some of the men whom, previously, he had commanded. He exchanged his captaincy for the position of Lieutenant-Colonel in the Coldstream Guards in May, 1758, and then drew up an elaborate list of instructions for his officers. Together with Lieutenant-Colonel Elliott he raised the first two regiments of horse in August, 1759. [32, 34] He went on the army expedition to Belle Ile off the coast of France in April, 1761; and, in March, 1762, he was sent to Portugal in command of an anglo-Portuguese brigade. In August of that year, he distinguished himself by capturing Valencia, and his Commander-in-Chief, Count le Lippe, wrote of his "remarkable valour, conduct and presence of mind", and recommended him to Lord Bute as "a most excellent officer, extremely worthy of his Majesty's remembrance." He was promoted to Colonel in the following October, and according to Lord Bute, this was done "out of regard to Lord Strange", as well as for his own merit. [34]

John's political career began in 1760. He was offered a seat in Parliament by one of the officers in his regiment, Sir William Peere Williams, and was returned unopposed in the election of 1761. The Duke of Newcastle had not approved of his nomination in the first instance, but had been assured by the Lord of the Admiralty, Hans Stanley, that John would "honourably and steadily adhere to every assurance he gives to your Grace on this occasion". [34] Newcastle left the Government in the spring of 1762, and Lord Bute took over for a year, until George Grenville replaced him in 1763, and was left to deal with problems both at home and in the North American Colonies. John supported Grenville's administration until the question of the infamous Stamp Act came up. Stamp duties were proposed for collection of taxes from the Americans to help to pay for the army provided for their defence, after land-hungry colonists began to take over lands which, previously belonged to French and Spanish settlers, as well as to the North American Indians. The British taxpayer was over-burdened with taxes due to the Seven Years' War, and money was short. The Act was passed in March, 1765, without taking into consideration American views on it, and representations made by some Members of Parliament. [40, 41] Burgoyne was one of the forty-nine Members who voted against it, but two hundred and forty-five votes had been given to approve it. The news arrived in America in April 1765 and the subsequent violent reaction eventually led to Grenville's dismissal and the repeal of the Act in the following year. [34, 40, 41]

Between 1765 and 1768, John Burgoyne only made one speech in the Commons, and this took place on 3rd February, 1766, in respect of legislation in Ireland. In the autumn of the same year, he went to Germany to study the battlefields of the Seven Years' War, and attended some army manoeuvres in Austria. Afterwards, he wrote a paper entitled *Observations and reflections upon the present military state of Prussia,* and presented it to Lord Chatham, whose administration had his support. He voted for them over the Land Tax Bill in February, 1767. [34]

In 1768, John was chosen by his brother-in-law, Lord Strange, to fight the Preston election, together with Sir Henry Hoghton, on behalf of the Whig Party. It was one of the most violent elections of the century. The returning-officers rejected the claims of many permanent residents in this "freeman borough" who said they had a right to vote, and the

Interior of dining-room at The Oaks. Design attributed to Sir Robert Taylor, the architect employed by John Burgoyne in 1770. RCHME Crown Copyright.

two Tory candidates were elected. Lord Strange claimed that by a resolution approved by the House of Commons in 1661, all male inhabitants of age in Preston "had voices" in parliamentary elections. He had recorded how the rejected voters would have voted, and his figures showed that the Whigs had defeated the Tory candidates by five hundred and eighty votes. After he had argued his case before the Commons, it was upheld, and Burgoyne and Hoghton took their seats in Parliament. However, as a result of John's actions at the hustings, he was tried in 1769 for incitement to violence. At his trial, he admitted that he had gone to the poll with a guard of soldiers, and loaded pistols. As a result, he had to pay a fine of £1,000, and was fortunate to escape imprisonment. Although he made seventy speeches in the House during his term of office as a Member, unlike his brother-in-law, he never gained a reputation as a speaker. [33, 34]

More criticism was aimed at John in respect of his army career, when he was made the Governor of Fort William under suspicious circumstances. It was most unusual for someone with the rank of colonel of a regiment to gain this position without first becoming a major-general - but John's good family connections could have played an important part in his promotion. [34] By May 1772, he had been promoted to Major-General.

Because of the forceful means by which he gained his seat in Parliament, John tried to be a successful Member. On 13th April, 1772, he moved for a Select Committee to be formed to examine the East India Company's affairs, and became the Committee's Chairman. They investigated the events in India since 1757 and, although their findings had a considerable influence on the opinion of the House, these did not affect the Government's policy. John's aim was to rob Lord Clive of his wealth. On 10th May, 1772, resolutions were passed condemning the conduct of the Company's employees in India; but the vote of censure on Clive was defeated. John resented the lack of support by the administration, and his resentment continued throughout the next three years, so that by 1774 he was on bad terms with Lord North. However, he supported his Administration's policy towards the American colonies, [34] where the unsympathetic handling of affairs, and further taxation imposed after the repeal of the Stamp Act, were causing more unrest. [40, 41]

Despite the fact that John had become a dandy, a convivial drinker and a gambler, and was a charming, colourful man about London town, he was not without talent. [41] During the period of criticism about his army career, and the frustration he felt over his political one, he turned his attention to his love of artistic matters. By now, he had acquired a town-house at 10, Hertford Street in Mayfair, and, between 1769 and 1771, he employed Robert Adam to decorate the interior of his London residence. The ceilings and friezes in the dining -room, ante-room, back parlour and two drawing-rooms were decorated, and chimney pieces were added to all of these rooms, with the exception of one drawing room. The decorations were completed in 1771, when the mirrors were installed, and, probably, the work here was an interesting example of Adam's "transition period". [42]

John also was involved with the architect, Sir Robert Taylor, and built 3 Grafton Street for Lord Howe. Sir Robert designed 4 Grafton Street as well. In about 1770, John's work began on Lambert's Oaks, where he added a magnificent dining-room to the eastern side of it, which has been attributed to Taylor, and should not be confused with Adam's later designs for the house. The room was forty-two feet in length, including the arched recesses at each end; twenty-one feet in width, and eighteen feet high. There were twenty-six small-cased Corinthian columns with a cornice, and various medallions on the walls. The design here was very similar in style to that of a ground-floor room at 4 Grafton Street, and to the short columns in the Court Room at the Bank of England - both examples of Taylor's work. [43] Locally, the interior of the Blue Room at Carshalton House also has similar blank wall arcading and, again, may be by Taylor.

It has been conjectured that John Burgoyne made additions to Lambert's Oaks, with Sir Robert Taylor, at this time, such as the dining-room on the east side, and a kitchen wing on the west of the house, [31] which would mean the completion of the building as designed originally by Sir Robert for the probable previous tenant, Sir Thomas Gosling. Perhaps Sir Thomas only rebuilt the main block of Lambert's Oaks before giving up his lease. Allegedly, John also made some improvements to the grounds around the house.[39]

In 1771, John gave up his lease on Lambert's Oaks, and it was taken over by his father-in-law, Lord Derby. [9] In the same year, John's best friend, Lord Strange, died of apoplexy while he was on a visit to Bath in June, 1771. His untimely death left his eldest son, Lord Edward Smith Stanley, as the Earl's new heir before he had reached the age of nineteen. The Earl, who was then eighty years old, took over again the duties of Lord-Lieutenant of Lancashire, and lived long enough to see his grandson make a prestigious marriage, the beginning of a political career, and the development of his inherited love of horse-racing, cock-fighting and life in high society. [33]

Young Lord Edward's education began at Preston Grammar School, and, between the years 1764 and 1770, he went to Eton, then on to Cambridge, where he matriculated at Trinity College, and received his Master of Arts Degree in 1773. He was at the university at the time of his father's death, and, after that, his uncle, John Burgoyne, became his close friend and confidant. [36]

Life at university was not dedicated entirely to studies, because at nearby Newmarket young Lord Edward could take part in the race-meetings and balls held there, as well as other diversions such as the gaming tables, cock-fighting and drinking. [36] After completing his academic (and sporting) education, he invariably acted as a steward at the races on the Downs at Epsom, [22] which suggests that he also spent a good deal of his time at Lambert's Oaks with his grandfather during the sporting seasons, and, probably, began to use the house on more occasions than the aging Lord Derby.

Lord Edward purchased a town-house at No. 23 (later No. 26) Grosvenor Square, which became known as Derby House. Possibly through his uncle John's influence, he

Interior of dining-room at The Oaks, showing detail of Corinthian capitals, with both semi-circular and rectangular fluted pilasters at the junction of the main body of the dining-room with the apse (to the right). The entablature is fairly plain.
RCHME Crown copyright.

loyed Robert Adam to design a new suite of rooms there. Adam's drawings for the
 e bear the dates of 1773 and 1774. Young Lord Stanley's addiction to the lavish
 vities, in which the richer members of society took part at that time, made him
 atient to show off his newly-acquired property to his friends. Consequently, as soon
 he decorations commenced, he decided to hold a fashionable reception here, and the
 nished condition of the rooms was cleverly concealed from the guests by the work of
 'upholsterers".[42]

 prolific writer of letters at that time, Horace Walpole, attended these festivities; and,
 is witty, critical style, wrote a detailed description of them in a letter to the Countess
 Jpper Ossory. Apparently, it was a very expensive affair, "for it is the fashion now to
 e romances rather than balls". A band of French horns and clarinets, whose players
 e dressed in "laced uniforms", provided the musical entertainment in the entrance hall,
 re coloured glass lanterns illuminated the dome of the staircase. There was a "bevy of
 als in white habits" making tea in the ante-room; also the unfinished state of the
 se was disguised by draperies of sarcenet, some of which were hung "with a very
 ereal air" across a chimney, and festooned over the sconces. The ballroom "was
 ned into an oval with benches above each other, not unlike pews". These were
 ered "with red serge", and over them were "arbours of flowers, red and green pilasters,
 e sarcenet, and Lord March's glass", on loan to the host, because "an upholsterer had
 ed Lord Stanley for £300 for the loan of same". One wall had been "burst open" to
 ommodate an orchestra, whose musicians were dressed in scarlet robes, "like the
 dle snuffers who represent the senates of Venice at Drury Lane", and the dancers were
 ected in a pendant mirror.[42]

 ortunately, Horace Walpole was unable to reach two more rooms due to the density of
 large crowds of people gathered there, but he was able to see the entertainments
 vided by the host for his guests. "The Seasons" were danced by Lord Stanley, "the
 nger Storer, the Duc de Lauzen and another", as well as "the youngest Miss Stanley,
 s Poole, the youngest Wrottesley, and another Miss", whose name the scribe could not
 all. The ladies were dressed as shepherdesses, except for the Misses Storer and
 ottesley, who wore "banians [loose morning gowns or jackets] with fur, for winter,
 k and hen". Also, what were described as "magnificent suppers" were served in the
 rooms below. [42]

 s sumptuous reception given by Lord Stanley was the first of many festive occasions
 d at his town-house. As time progressed, his residence here became the centre of
 idon's social life. [36] Robert Adam's interior decorations at Derby House were,
 obably, the masterpieces of his similar works in London". [42] Also, he was involved
 h some work at Lambert's Oaks in the following years.

Chapter 4
A FAMOUS FÊTE AND A RELUCTANT BRIDE

Young Lord Stanley was one of the most eligible bachelors in the Georgian society of 1773. He had hoped to marry the Duchess of Bedford's niece, but she declined his offer of marriage. By the end of that year, he had fallen in love with Lady Elizabeth (Betty) Hamilton, who was the daughter of the Duchess of Argyll. She was a little younger than Lord Edward, having been born at Holyrood Palace in Edinburgh on 26th January, 1753, and was the eldest child of James, the sixth Duke of Hamilton and his Duchess, the Lady Elizabeth. [36] Before her marriage, Betty's mother had been one of the two celebrated beauties, the Gunning sisters, and when they first appeared in London, Maria was eighteen years old and Elizabeth seventeen. The older girl became Lady Coventry, but died at an early age due to consumption, allegedly aggravated by the cosmetics which she used, while her sister made two good marriages and lived to be a great age. [44]

After leading a rather hectic life of extravagant gambling and dissipation, Betty's father, the Duke of Hamilton, died in 1758, before he reached his thirty-fourth birthday. He had been a competent horseman, and usually rode his own race-horses; also he was a member of the Jockey Club. Baron Mure was one of the principal guardians of the Duke's children, and just over one year after her husband's death, the widow married again and became the Duchess of Argyll. [36, 44]

Lord Stanley and Lady Betty became engaged during the early months of 1774, but it was alleged that he showed more interest in her than she did in him. Previously, her admirers had been the Marquis of Carmallen, the Duke of Devonshire, and John Frederick Sackville, the Duke of Dorset's heir. Lady Betty had fallen in love with the good-looking John Sackville, who, already, had gained quite a reputation with the ladies. Therefore, the Duchess of Argyll did not entirely approve of him as a suitor for her daughter, and was anxious to make for her what was considered to be one of the best matches in the whole of England. Thus, she was delighted when young Lord Edward proposed marriage to Betty, and, eventually, persuaded her to accept him. [36]

The young couple decided upon a June wedding, and in honour of his prospective bride, Lord Edward planned to hold what became the most famous party given at The Oaks. The Fête Champêtre (rural feast, or festival) took place on Thursday, 9th June, 1774, [44] and excited great interest because it was the first of its kind to be held in England. [13] Lord Edward's uncle, John Burgoyne, made all of the arrangements for the Fête, and Robert Adam was employed to design a temporary pavilion to be erected in the gardens of the house.[44]

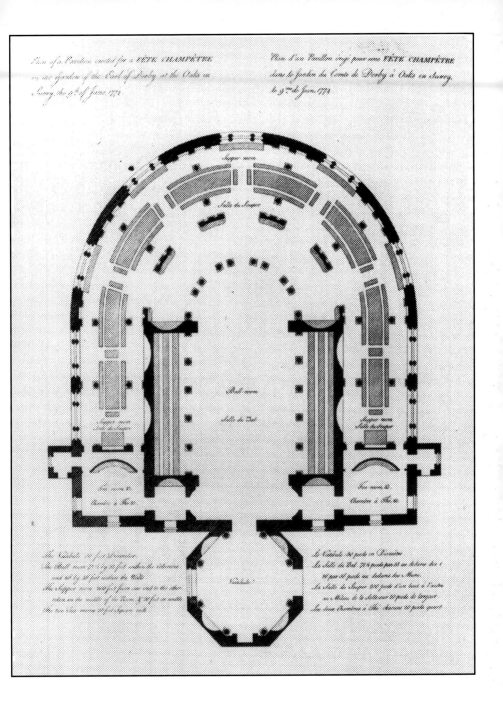

Plan of the temporary pavilion designed by Robert Adam for the Féte champétre at Lambert's Oaks on 9th June 1774.

Robert Adam produced one of his best designs for the pavilion, and its origins can be traced from his own early studies and ideas during his time in Rome. It was approximately one hundred and forty feet in length from the front of the vestibule to the farthest end of the building, and one hundred feet in width. The ballroom in the centre of it was ninety feet long and sixty feet wide. A supper-room extended around most of its exterior, except for two tea rooms at each end of it, where access to them could be gained by the guests as they entered the main area (see plan). [44]

All of the rooms in the pavilion were superbly decorated throughout. The octagonal vestibule had transparent, painted windows at each end, and crimson curtains with a deep gold fringe on them. There were colonnades with wreaths of flowers running up them on each side of the ballroom, which was lined "chairback high with a white Persian and gold fringe". The seats around this room were covered with deep crimson. [45]

Although Horace Walpole did not attend the Fête, he wrote to Sir Thomas Mann on the day before the event took place, and commented on Lord Stanley's marriage later in that month, as well as on the festivities planned for the prospective bride: "... he gives her a most splendid entertainment at his villa (the Oaks at Epsom) in Surrey and calls it a 'fête champêtre'. It will cost £5,000. Everybody is to go in masquerade, but not in mask. He has bought all the orange trees around London, and the haycocks, I suppose, are to be made of straw-coloured satin."[44]

As well as supervising the arrangements for his nephew's Fête, John Burgoyne wrote a "sylvan masque" especially for the occasion. It provided part of the entertainment for the guests at the beginning of the evening, and was performed in the garden of The Oaks. [45] François Barthélemon, the leader of the orchestra at the Vauxhall pleasure gardens, composed the music for the play.[36]

Approximately three hundred members of the "principal nobility" had been invited to attend the Fête in fancy dress. [13] On the day of the festivities, it was alleged that Lord North, the Prime Minister, found it difficult to muster a quorum in the House of Commons, because so many Members were preparing for their journeys to The Oaks. [36] On arrival, the guests left their carriages and walked through the gate on to the front lawn, where they were greeted by "carefully concealed French horns". The lawn soon became crowded, and the ladies had the opportunity to observe each others' fancy, pastoral dresses. Orders had been given for the gate leading on to the downs to be opened, so that the large crowds of spectators could see some of the proceedings, as well as the people who had been invited to the Fête. [45]

If Horace Walpole had been present on this splendid occasion, there can be little doubt that he would have written a good description of the proceedings. However, another prolific writer of letters at that time, Mrs. Mary Delaney, was among the guests, and, afterwards, she wrote to one of her relatives and gave an eye-witness account of the festivities. She described the event as "a fairy scene ... nothing at least in modern days has been exhibited so perfectly magnificent, everybody in good humour, and agreed that it exceeded their expectations." The "master" of the entertainment, Lord Stanley, "was dressed like Rubens, and Lady Betty Hamilton (for whom the feast was made) like Rubens' wife." [44] (Another source of information said that they wore Flemish costume after the style of Van Dyck.) [36] The lawn in front of The Oaks was scattered with trees "and opens to the downs". The parties of people of all ranks, who came to watch the proceedings, "made the scene quite enchanting, which was greatly enlivened with a most beautiful sun breaking from a black cloud in its greatest glory." [44]

At about 8 p.m., a signal was given for the guests to attend the Masque on the back lawn, and they were led there by General Burgoyne. On their way, their attention was drawn to the crowds of people on either side of the road, and in the trees. At the upper end of the lawn was an orangery, or plantation of orange trees, intermixed with a great variety of greenhouse plants. The orangery concealed Mr. Barthélemon's musicians; also other entertainments here were provided by "swains in fancy dress" playing nine-pins, or with bows and arrows shooting at a bird perched on a maypole, while others danced and kicked at a "tambour de Basque" decorated with ribbons and hung from a tree, and shepherdesses were on some swings. Mrs. Barthélemon and a Mr. Vernon were in the centre of the orangery making wreaths of flowers until the guests were seated on the benches, which had been placed in a circle on the lawn. Then two cupids with baskets of flowers presented each lady with a bouquet, and the gentlemen were given similar presents. [45]

The Sylvan Masque began with Mr. Vernon calling upon the nymphs and shepherds to celebrate the festivity of the day, informing them that their host, as Lord of The Oaks, invited them to join in the songs and dances which followed. Mrs. Barthélemon and Mr. Vernon sang a duet, and Mr. Vernon's solo with choruses was accompanied by the dance of the Sylvans. [45] Mrs. Delaney described the Masque and said that the guests were welcomed by a dialogue "between a shepherd and shepherdess" given from the garden stage. "It was said, sung and danced by sixteen pairs of men and women dancers from the opera", and lasted for about half an hour. Afterwards, "swinging, jumping, archery and country sports took place until it was dark."[44]

After the entertainments had finished, the guests walked around until a signal was given for them to form another procession which was led by Lord Edward Stanley and Lady Betty Hamilton (as Queen of The Oaks) and accompanied by the band of musicians. They went to the other side of the garden and into the pavilion, which Mrs. Delaney described as "a magnificent saloon ... illuminated and decorated with the utmost elegance and proportion". The ball began here and lasted until 11.30 p.m., then an "explosion" was heard as the signal for the crimson curtains to be raised to expose the supper-room with tables spread with the "most costly dainties, all hot and tempting". Everyone quickly took their seats. Mrs. Delaney enjoyed the food and commented that it was "exceedingly good, and everybody glad of it" because the evening's entertainments had commenced "so early". After the dessert had been served and consumed, the band began playing again,

Interior of the temporary pavilion designed by Robert Adam for the fête champêtre, showing part of the supper room. From an engraving by J. Caldwall and C. Grignion.

and everyone adjourned to the ballroom, where General Burgoyne arranged them into a circular group around Lady Betty, and the next part of the festival commenced. [44, 45]

Lord March, in the role of one of the Druids, supposedly inhabitants of The Oaks, welcomed Lady Betty, and told her that Lord Stanley was happy and fortunate to have her as a prospective bride. He then prophesied happiness for their marriage, and some dryads, Cupid and Hymen danced and sang choruses. This section of the proceedings concluded with the "Happiness of the Oak", a tree which formed part of the Hamilton coat of arms. A piece of transparent painting was brought in depicting the crests of the Hamilton and Stanley families surrounded by emblems of Cupid and Hymen, and it was crowned with a wreath of flowers. [44] Afterwards, the second ball began with music composed by the Earl of Kelly, and Lord Edward and Lady Betty led the dancers on to the floor. All of the guests joined in the minuets, which were followed by country dancing lasting until beyond three o'clock in the morning. [45]

The guests also admired the illuminations in the gardens. A large Ionic portico supported by four transparent bright pink columns led out from the great room (the name by which John Burgoyne's dining-room was known) to the pavilion. The words "to Propitious Venus" were written on its transparent pediment, in the centre of which was a shield with the Stanley and Hamilton arms supported by a band of cupids and illuminated by four pyramids of light. Other pyramids of lights had been erected in different parts of the garden to provide more illuminations. [45] Mrs. Delaney was very impressed with the whole of the Fête, and remarked that everyone attending it was "very elegantly dressed, the very young as peasants, the next as Polonises; the matrons as dominos; the men principally dominos, and many gardiners, as in Opera dances."[44] (A polonise, or polonaise, was a woman's dress consisting of a bodice and short skirt in one piece; a domino was a masquerade dress worn by men and women consisting of a loose cloak or mantle, with a small mask.)

Such splendid entertainments would have overwhelmed any eager bride-to-be in her role as the principal guest. However, Lady Betty seemed to cope with the situation very well in the circumstances, and her mother, the Duchess of Argyll, looked upon the whole affair with approval and interest. The festivities continued throughout the night, and, when these had ended, some of the guests did not depart for several days afterwards. [36]

The Duchess of Bedford had refused her invitation to the Fête. Apparently, she was upset about the way in which young Lord Stanley had quickly recovered from her niece's refusal of his offer of marriage. Afterwards, the Duchess had some regrets at having missed the most important social gathering of that year. On 16th June, 1774, the Dowager Countess Gower wrote to Mrs. Delaney and informed her: "I was told today that the old hoydon, the Ds of Bedford, was not at Lord Stanley's Fête: I sopose piqu'd at his recovering her nieces refusal so soon, for she wd not let any of 'em go, tho all the Bloomsbury-gang was invited." (The Bloomsbury gang was composed of the Duke of Bedford's political followers.) Also, after hearing "how fine, charming and elegant it was", the Duchess's admission of regret over her decision to stay away from the festivities caused the Dowager Countess to comment: "she is silly enough to confess she repents, cd she had been silent, people might have thought she had commenced a decency suitable to her age."[44]

The Dowager Countess also told Mrs. Delaney: "Geo Selwyn says 'the fête appeared to him as if Col-Burgoyne had plan'd it and Lord Stanley paid for it.' " Furthermore, there was criticism about the fact that Lord March had acted as the speaker for the Druids, "wh Fame says was not very desent," and the Duchess of Argyll had remarked, "nothing but Betty could have stood it all!" [44] Possibly, the comments about Lord March's role in the festivities arose from the fact that he was well-known as the rowdiest member of the gang of men who supported the Prince of Wales in opposition to George III's ministers in the government at this time. [36]

A detailed description of the Fête appeared in the *Gentleman's Magazine* for June 1774, and a brief account of it was given in the *Annual Register* for the same year. Eventually, two engravings by J. Caldwall and C. Grignon of the interiors of the ball and supper rooms were published in 1780, and these showed the costumes worn by the guests, as well as the rich effect of Adam's architectural arrangements and decorations in the pavilion. [13]

The marriage between Lord Stanley and Lady Betty took place on Thursday, 23rd June, 1774. The event was described in a letter written on the following day by Andrew Stuart to one of Lady Betty's guardians, Baron Mure, who was not present on that occasion. Apparently, the lawyers had been very busy on the day before the wedding, and had worked through the Wednesday night, so that the marriage settlements could be signed at 2 p.m., before the ceremony took place. The schedule for the great day was: "Dinner at the Duchess of Argyll's between four and five. Marriage ceremony between seven and eight, and then set out for The Oaks." Mr Stuart also remarked: "I can only say that, in modern times, there are few instances of more ardent lovers than this young heir of the Derby race. He was highly sensible of Lady Betty's merit and personal attractions, and you never saw any lover more impatient of delays than he has been." [44] Such a remark suggests that the bride had been reluctant to agree upon a date on which to marry her eager bridegroom!

The wedding was a quiet affair and the only guests in attendance at the ceremony were Lord Archibald Hamilton, who gave the bride away, Lady Charlotte Edwin, two of Lord Stanley's sisters, General Burgoyne and Mr. Stuart. [44] The decorations at the bridegroom's town-house in Grosvenor Square were not completed by that time; therefore Lord Edward and Lady Betty Stanley spent their honeymoon at The Oaks. Soon after their marriage, King George III and Queen Charlotte visited them there, and, a little later, Lady Betty was invited to supper with them at Kew House.[36]

In September, 1774, Lord Stanley's uncle, John Burgoyne, reluctantly had to leave his wife, Lady Charlotte, who was now an invalid, when he was ordered to Canada with

Interior of the temporary pavilion designed by Robert Adam for the fête champêtre, showing part of the supper room. From an engraving by J.Caldwall and C. Grignion.

the army, due to the unrest in the American colonies. [32] The masque he had written for the Fête Champêtre was included in his play, *The Maid of the Oaks,* which David Garrick produced at the Drury Lane Theatre on 5th November 1774, and included choruses and dances of shepherdesses, gardeners, carpenters, painters and village maidens, Act I began with the hero, Sir Harry Groveby, welcoming his friend, Charles Dupely, to an ornamented farm owned by a Mr. Oldworth, who was the guardian of Maria (the Maid of The Oaks). Sir Harry tells Charles of his forthcoming marriage to Maria, after their separation for a period of six months undertaken at Mr. Oldworth's insistence. Dupely tries, unsuccessfully, to convince Sir Harry that Maria is similar to all women, but is informed that she is superior to them. Hurry, a servant, then confirms Sir Harry's opinion before he leaves to continue with the preparations for a Fête Champêtre.[46]

The second scene (The Oaks) opens with a song by Maria, before Mr. Oldworth appears and tells her he will grant her any wish she has left. She informs him of her apprehension about her unknown origins, but he assures her that these will be revealed during that evening. He then welcomes Lady Bab Lardoon before Sir Harry appears and receives Lady Bab's congratulations: also she tells him that she has lost two thousand guineas at the gaming tables. Mr. Oldworth says that Charles Dupely has arrived, and she offers to meet him and take the opportunity to tell him she could make an example of his hypocrisy, as well as "his graces and image de monde."[46]

Act II begins with a short scene, "The Garden Gate", in which Sir Harry's uncle, Old Grovely, informs him of his disapproval of the marriage because of Maria's unknown origins. He threatens to return to his home, Groomstock Hall, and alter his will. However, he meets Maria in the next scene, "A Grove", but as neither of them knows each other's identity, he asks her about the bride, and they agree that it is an uneven match. He informs her that he has come to break it up because the groom is his nephew. Maria leaves the stage, and the bridegroom joins his uncle. Old Grovely complains that Mr. Oldworth has not contacted him, and is making a fool of Sir Harry. Thus, he is tempted to take the sensible young lady whom he has just met, and return to Groomstock Hall to hold his own Champêtre wedding. Sir Harry's suspicions are aroused, and after questioning his uncle about the lady, he informs him that she was Maria. [46]

In the third scene, "A Flower Garden", Lady Bab appears dressed as a shepherdess. Mr. Oldworth points out Charles Dupely to her and she introduces herself to him as "Philly Nettletop",who is one of the bridesmaids, before talking sarcastically about "fine gentlemen". She informs him that Lady Bab will be attending the Fête, and he replies that he would rather be in love with "the figure of the great mogul at the back of a pack of cards", and tries to kiss "Philly". Sir Harry appears and addresses her as Lady Bab, thus revealing her true identity!

The play ends on a happy note, because Mr. Oldworthy reveals that Maria is his daughter, and an heiress, and Dupely proposes to Lady Bab. [46] A special performance of it took place afterwards, by the royal command of King George III and Queen Charlotte, [36] but opinions differed in respect of the play's success. The actors and actresses who took part in these first productions included a Mrs. Baddely as Maria. Mrs. Abingdon was the fashionable Lady Bab Lardoon; the hero, Sir Harry Grovely, was played by Mr. Palmer; and Mr. Dodd was Charles Dupely. [46]

Meanwhile, work continued on the Stanley's town-house in Grosvenor Square. Adam's scheme and style for the suites of rooms was a requisite background for the members of Georgian society, who would be entertained here at many future receptions given by the owner. The whole effect was complemented by fine painted furniture, mirrors, mantelpieces and other decorations. It was an appropriate setting for the newly-weds, and the design for the picture in the centre of the ceiling in the bedroom depicted *Night sowing Poppies,* while Lady Betty's "Bow Dressing-room" was decorated with Adam's Etruscan designs. [42]

Lord Stanley became a member of the Jockey Club in 1774, and was elected to the membership of White's, the oldest and most exclusive of London's clubs. [36] He commenced his political career in the same year, when he was returned unopposed for Lancashire, where one seat in the House of Commons was usually conceded to his family.[34] By December, 1774, the ageing eleventh Earl of Derby had decided to give up his racing and hunting seat in Surrey, and he handed it over to his grandson. On 6th February, 1775, Lord Edward took over the house, [47] which was then known as "the Oaks near Epsom" because of Epsom's previous importance, and the fact that Woodmansterne was only a small, less well-known village at that time.

The owner of The Oaks, young William Lambert, was fourteen years old when Lord Stanley took over the lease of it. William's two surviving guardians, John Ebbutt, a gentleman of St. Mary Cray, and Thomas Peter, a maltster of Leatherhead, were involved in this transaction. Lord Stanley's lease was for a term of eighty-three and one quarter years from Christmas Day, 1774, until Lady Day, 1858. He paid a yearly rent of £25 for the estate comprised of just over three acres of enclosed "wood-ground" with the house in it; a piece of land between the new highway from Croydon to Epsom, and the "ground" called The Oaks, which, previously, had been allotted to John Lambert, [47] (young William's father, who had died in 1771) [9] and his heirs, by the Justices of the Peace in lieu of, and as compensation for, about two acres over which the highway ran on the southern side of the property; also all other lands which Lord Stanley had enclosed there. One of the conditions of the lease stated that the new tenant and his heirs could cut down for their own benefit any of the trees, woods and undergrowth with the exception of the beech trees, and these were not to be destroyed. [47]

On 21st April, 1775, a son and heir, another Edward Smith Stanley, was born to Lord Edward and Lady Betty. [32] The proud father decided to hold a regatta on the Thames to celebrate his son's birth, and the party took place on the evening of 23rd June, 1775. It was intended to outdo the Fête Champêtre at The Oaks, but, due to the unpredictable weather (even in those days) these festivities had been postponed three times because of

Edward, 12th Earl of Derby with his first wife, Elizabeth (Betty), and their son Edward painted by Angelica Kauffman. ©A Private collection, copyright reserved.

the rainfall! Eventually, a flag was flown from Westminster Bridge on 23rd June, as a signal to everyone invited to attend it that the party would take place on that day. It attracted crowds of people along both banks of the river, as well as on the roof-tops along the course of the main event, which was a boat-race between twelve pair-oar boats rowing from Westminster Bridge to London Bridge, and back again. The large numbers of guests followed the race in wherries and barges, which were decorated in a similar style to the boats used by the Doges of Venice, and the competitors were given shouts of encouragement from these spectators. Afterwards, Lord and Lady Stanley took the guests to the Ranelagh Pleasure Gardens, where they dined and danced until the early hours of the next morning. [36]

Lady Betty had been under the strict influence of her mother throughout most of the first year of her marriage to Lord Stanley, but now she began to break away from the Duchess of Argyll. As a result, some of Betty's friends, who were invited to the regatta, did not meet with the Duchess's approval, because their previous escapades had made them the objects of gossip. Very soon, her own daughter's improprieties were causing the Duchess much concern! [36]

Lord Edward also became involved in political matters, and had spoken for the first time in the House of Commons on 24 January, 1775. His maiden speech met with much approval, and Horace Walpole mentioned it in one of his letters to the Countess of Upper Ossory, and wrote that his lordship has "pleased by his manner, his matter, they say, would have pleased as well on any other day". Stanley was a strong supporter of British rights over the American colonies, where events were leading up to the War of Independence, and he voted against Lord North's conciliation proposals on 20th February, 1775. His two other speeches in the Commons, on 16th October and 1st December in the same year, were about affairs in Lancashire. [34]

The Stanley's town-house in Grosvenor Square had become a centre of social activities, and it was considered to be the ultimate sign of social success to receive an invitation to dine, dance, or spend an evening at cards there. Charles Fox was among those who frequented the gaming tables, and Lady Betty, who was very fond of whist, spent hours playing for high stakes. [36] On Tuesday, 19th December, 1775, Selwyn wrote to Lord Carlisle: "Last night and the night before, I supped at Lady Betty Stanley's. Their suppers are magnificent, but their hours are abominably late..." Also some of the guests went off to a masquerade at 2 am! [42] Although outwardly the young couple's marriage seemed successful, their private life was not a very happy one.

Chapter 5
AN UNFINISHED CASTLE, A CRICKET MATCH AND A DEFEATED GENERAL

During the first half of 1776, the Stanley family suffered three bereavements. The eleventh Earl of Derby's death occurred at Knowsley on 22nd February, 1776. His widow, Elizabeth, died two days later, and both of them were buried in the Derby Chapel at Ormskirk.33 Young Lord Edward inherited the earldom and its wealth, and a seat in the House of Lords. King George III then appointed him as the Lord-Lieutenant of Lancashire, which was an office held by all the preceding Earls, and, as the title-holder, he automatically became the commander-in-chief of that county's militia. The late Lord Derby also bequeathed £25,000, and an annuity of £500, to his daughter, Lady Charlotte Burgoyne. [32, 34] Unfortunately, still in a state of ill health, she did not survive her father for many more months, and died in June, 1776, when John Burgoyne was with the army in Canada.

The twelfth Earl of Derby used The Oaks for his sporting activities and entertained his guests there throughout his life. By February, 1776, Robert Adam's interior decorations at Derby House in Grosvenor Square had been completed. The young Earl immediately employed him to produce some sketches for alterations to Knowsley, and, probably at this time, schemes for The Oaks. The Adam designs for the Earl's sporting seat are not well-known. None was published in the life-times of either Robert or James Adam, and were reproduced for the first time in 1985. [31]

Robert Adam made four separate designs for rebuilding The Oaks. It is estimated that the costs of building from these designs would have ranged from £11,000 for a large, rectangular house with elaborate baronial wings, to £5,404:5s:0d. for a square castle set between miniature pavilions. None of these schemes was used, and they were all undated, but it has been conjectured that the date could have been around 1777. A part, only, of a fifth scheme was used, which was almost exactly contemporary with the first stage of Adam's work at Culzean Castle in Ayrshire begun in February, 1777. It included a canted-bay addition on to the south-west front of The Oaks, and a castle-style extension, measuring forty by thirty-three feet, built on to the southern end of John Burgoyne's dining-room on the south-eastern side. This new saloon, or drawing-room, had a range of three windows on the eastern and western walls, and a Venetian window on the south. The paired turrets on either side of the Venetian window, the low triple window above it, together with the cross-slit windows and corner bartizans (or projecting turrets), are typical of Adam's work. [31]

Other work carried out at The Oaks was a re-casing of the older house, thus retaining the magnificent dining-room added by the Earl's uncle, John Burgoyne, as well as Sir Robert Taylor's earlier design for most of the centre of the building. However, all work ceased when two thirds of it was completed, and this leads to more conjectures about Lord Derby's decision to leave The Oaks in its unfinished state, as no further work was carried out during his life.[31] Possibly, because he was able to give his wife all of the luxuries his ample wealth could provide for her, he had decided to present Betty with a lavish, small castle as a romantic setting for their sumptuous entertainments held at their country residence. As events showed, and before the work was completed, he found he had been betrayed by his Countess, and, therefore, decided not to proceed with his plans.

Although their marriage was not a very happy one, the young Earl and his Countess remained in royal favour, and, when their first daughter was born, she was sponsored by the King and Queen, and allowed to bear the Queen's name of Charlotte. Lord Derby's unhappy married life did not prevent him from enjoying his social and sporting events, and his love of horse-racing and cock-fighting increased. He and his wife continued to give their sumptuous parties and entertainments at their town-house in Grosvenor Square, and Betty's passion increased for her games of cards and balls, her assemblies, and her late hours. [36]

After the Declaration of Independence by the American colonies on 4th July, 1776, the war with America had little or no effect on the continual round of social activities enjoyed by the Earl, his wife, and other people included in their circle of friends. In a letter to Horace Mann on 18th June, 1777, Horace Walpole commented: "It is the fashion now to go to Ranelagh two hours after it is over. You may not believe this but it is literal. The music ends at ten, the company goes at twelve." He also informed his friend that Lord Derby's cook had complained to his employer that, although he liked working for him, "he should be killed by dressing suppers at three in the morning. The Earl asked him coolly how much he valued his life; that is he would have paid for killing him. You see, we have brought the spirit of calculation to perfection." [36] Apparently, Mr. Walpole did not approve of the interior decorations designed by Robert Adam for the Earl's town-house, and, in another letter written on 8th August, 1777, he described these as: "filligreed into puerility", and called the house "I'Hotel de Derby".48

In the summer of 1777, Lord and Lady Derby entertained some of their friends at The Oaks, and a two-day cricket match between Coulsdon and Chertsey was held here. The star performer of the Coulsdon team was the handsome John Frederick Sackville, by then the Duke of Dorset, who, at the age of thirty-seven, was an expert bowler and a keen supporter of, and player for, the Kent county team. Also, in 1777, the Duke was the captain of the Coulsdon Cricket Club, which, in those days when matches were played for stakes, and betting took place on the results, attracted members of the aristocracy. Dukes, Earls and Lords either played for, or against, this club whose home ground was situated on a triangular piece of land called Lion Green bounded by the present-day Brighton Road, Chipstead Valley Road and Lion Green Road. Refreshments and meals were served at the Red Lion Inn, where the stakes and wagers were paid. When Lord

Derby and his sporting friends came here, they used the bridleway which began opposite the grounds of The Oaks and led across the downs to Coulsdon. [49, 50]

The cricket match at The Oaks had disastrous effects on Lord Derby's marriage, and, possibly, led to the reason for the unfinished state of the Earl's castle here. Previously, John Sackville had treated Lady Betty's engagement with indifference, and he had been a guest at the Fête Champêtre. Afterwards, he had enticed the mistress of the Duke of Grafton, the notorious Nancy Parsons, into his protection in 1775, and had spent about two years in Europe. Georgiana, the Duchess of Devonshire, described him as "the most dangerous of men", because of his good looks, "unaffectedness and persuasion of his manner", and the fact that quite a number of ladies had been in love with him. On meeting the Countess of Derby again at the cricket match, he realised that her love for him had remained unchanged. [36]

The visiting team won the match at The Oaks on the second day, and then it was suggested that the ladies should play cricket. Betty, Lady Derby, who had a sense of fun, agreed to this suggestion, and, when the sides had been chosen, the teams came out on to the lawn. They wore "summer dresses of sprigged muslin or coloured lutestring without hoops or panniers, but with mob caps over their tall coiffures." Among the players were the Countess of Essex, the Countesses of Carlisle and Eglington, as well as their hostess and "a dozen other ladies of the first rank". Lady Derby, "who was as agile as a kitten, batted and bowled as dexterously as the best of them", and certainly won the admiration of the Duke of Dorset as well. Although the incident was not reported in the newspapers of that time, the Duke was so impressed, that he described the game in a letter to a friend, and "depicted the contest in a water colour drawing", which has been kept in the pavilion at Lord's Cricket Ground. [36]

The liaison between Betty and the Duke of Dorset was renewed after the cricket match. The fact that she was married gave her the added attraction now of being theoretically unobtainable - and the Duke's aim was conquest! Although he tried to be discreet by seeking Lord Derby's friendship, the affair did not remain a secret for very long, because he took advantage of every favourable opportunity to be at Betty's side, whispering avowals of his passion for her. Consequently, when her third child, Elizabeth Henrietta, was born, the gossips of that time circulated a rumour that she was the Duke's daughter.[36]

In the spring of 1778, the mobilisation of the militia of several counties took place, because of fears of invasion from France - the ally of the American colonies in their War of Independence. As Colonel of the Lancashire Regiment, Lord Derby went to camp at Winchester with his men. Lady Derby, together with a group of her friends, made plans to camp nearby, so that they could be with their husbands. However, they were forbidden to go there by the War Minister. Betty's decision to stay in Brighthelmstone (Brighton) instead, soon led to the circulation of another rumour that Lord Derby and his wife had quarrelled because of his jealousy about the Duke of Dorset's attentions given to her. The

Earl and his Countess were last seen together at a party they gave at Derby House in May, 1778, when they appeared to be a devoted couple. [36]

By December, 1778, further rumours had been circulated that the Earl was about to divorce his Countess, so that she could marry the Duke of Dorset. The Duchess of Argyll attempted to seek a reconciliation between Lord Derby and her daughter, but she was unsuccessful. Derby did not intend to apply for the necessary Act of Parliament to enable him to divorce Lady Derby, but, instead, he insisted that she leave England for a few years, and, thus, prevent any further embarrassment to them both if they should meet each other at social gatherings The Queen, and some of Betty's friends, drifted away from her, except for Lady Sarah Lennox, who had been divorced by her husband, Sir Charles Bunbury, under similar circumstances. [36]

Lady Derby spent approximately four years in Europe. She visited Spa in Belgium, and travelled to Italy, Switzerland, Germany and Austria. In Vienna, she was entertained by the Emperor, Joseph II, and the British Minister there, Sir Robert Keith, acted as her chaperon. She wrote to Lord Derby during this period, but her rejected husband failed to reply to any of her letters, and she concluded that he had no intention of resuming their marriage. Their three children were reared at the Earl's family seat at Knowsley in Lancashire. [36]

During the period in which Lord Derby's marriage broke up, his uncle, General Burgoyne, became seriously involved in the American War of Independence, which had disastrous effects on his army career. In the events leading up to the war, the King and his friends had been warned by the British General, Thomas Gage, who held Boston, that the Americans were not to be taken lightly, and he asked for reinforcements. His warning and request went unheeded. After the beginning of hostilities, the American troops tried, unsuccessfully, to conquer the Canadian province of Quebec, and their action forced the Government to send reinforcements to the Thirteen Colonies. However, the army and its command were divided into two sections, and two commanders-in-chief were established. Such action helped the Americans to win the Saratoga campaign, an alliance with France - and their independence. [40, 41]

After spending the winter months of 1776, and the beginning of 1777, in London, where he convinced George III that the army should move down from Canada to quell the American rebellion, John Burgoyne returned full of confidence to Quebec on 6th May, 1777. [40] He took his place as commander at the head of the army that would be moving southward into the American colonies. At St. John's, on 13th June, his small but formidable force consisted of eight thousand redcoats and Hessians (Germans), approximately one hundred and fifty French Canadians, one hundred Tories (Americans upholding the British cause) and four hundred North American Indians. His officers included his second-in-command, Major-General William Phillips, Major-General Baron von Riedesel, who was the senior officer among the German troops, and Brigadier-General Simon Fraser, Lord Lovat. [41]

Burgoyne's army, which was well-equipped with artillery, set out in warships and a variety of other boats, including canoes, across Lake Champlain towards Fort Ticonderoga, and landed near there on 1st July. Also, Lieutenant Colonel Barry St. Leger arrived in Oswego on 26th July with about nine hundred men, and met the Mohawk chief, Joseph Brant, who joined him with approximately one thousand Iroquois warriors. They marched eastward towards the Mohawk valley. Meanwhile, the commander-in-chief, General Howe, was in New York with an army of eighteen thousand men. He set sail with his troops, went out into the Atlantic on 24th July, and disappeared until 25th August, when he landed in Maryland. [41]

The Americans chose General Philip Schuyler to command their army against Burgoyne and St. Leger, but he had no troops to send to Ticonderoga to help defend his garrison which was put to flight. John Burgoyne's elation over his easy victory did not last long. He had orders to proceed to Albany, and knew that no important help would be sent to him during his march of seventy miles over bad roads and through thick forests before he reached there. He was impeded by his heavy artillery, and embarrassed by a lack of horses and oxen required to move his cannon and military gear. General Schuyler ordered thousands of trees to be felled across John's route, and even had streams diverted to cause more problems. [41]

John and his troops slowly progressed to the Hudson river by 29th July, and, after a short delay, he moved another seven miles along the Hudson's east bank to Fort Miller, where he waited for many weeks until his artillery and gear reached him. The tide of war was turning against him during this time. [41]

The militia of New England and New York turned out in large numbers to defend their homes, and, together with a contingent of Yankees (northern Americans), they threatened the British army's left flank. John Burgoyne began to worry about his line of communication to Canada if more supplies were required. He gave permission to Baron von Riedesel to raid Green Mountain country for more horses, oxen, wagons and food, and Colonel Friedrich Baum was sent off with seven hundred men, two cannon and a few artillery-men, with orders to avoid any heavy losses. After meeting a strong enemy force, he disobeyed orders and was mortally wounded at the battle of Bennington. The remnants of his troops either fled, or surrendered, before reinforcements under Lieutenant-Colonel Francis Breyman could reach them. The Americans regrouped their own reinforced troops, and defeated Breyman. The battle cost Burgoyne the loss of more than one tenth of his army in one day - and more bad news followed. [41]

Barry St. Leger had advanced along the Mohawk valley, and had been compelled to besiege Fort Stanwix. A rumour had been infiltrated and spread among St. Leger's Indians that three thousand Americans were advancing towards them - in truth, just over one thousand men. The Indians already had suffered some losses, and they fled through the forests. St. Leger had to retreat because, without the warriors, he could not maintain the siege. [41]

The American General Schuyler was replaced by General Horatio Gates. His troops were continually reinforced with more volunteers, and he established them at Benns Heights to await Burgoyne's arrival. On 18th September, 1777, John and his army camped three miles north of Gates's men, and went into action on the next day with attacks on the Americans' left wing, while Baron von Riedesel moved along the Hudson against their right flank. The first battle of Freeman's Farm (as it became known) ended in losses of about six hundred of John's men, whom he could ill-afford to lose. He was forced to withdraw, and lay quiet for nearly three weeks, during which time the morale of his officers and troops fell, and they were short of food. The Baron and Simon Fraser advised a retreat to Canada, but John resolved to try again to break through the American line. [41]

The second battle of Freeman's Farm also ended disastrously for John. He lost a further seven hundred men, either killed, wounded or captured. Whatever hopes he had of reaching Albany soon faded, and he withdrew to a good position near Saratoga. General Gates ordered his militia to cut off Burgoyne's route to Ticonderoga, and, when John decided to retreat to Canada, he found that his army was surrounded. [41]

On 13th October, 1777, John sent a message to General Gates offering to lay down his arms on suitable terms, but Gates demanded a complete surrender. The next day, John informed the General that his army would put down its weapons if the men were allowed to go back to Britain after pledging never to return to North America - and his terms were accepted. Burgoyne learned too late that British troops had been sent up the River Hudson, and were not far from Albany. He was tempted to resume fighting, but, being an officer and a gentleman, he decided not to withdraw his offer of surrender which had been accepted. He reached Albany at last - as a prisoner. His troops were led away to captivity and were not allowed to return to England. [41]

The news of John's surrender at Saratoga shook the British nation, not least Lord North's government. When John returned to England, he had to face severe criticism of his defeat, and he tried to defend himself in Parliament against attacks from nearly every party in the House. The Government denounced him for his failure. John Wilkes and his supporters attacked him for his allegedly brutal use of the 'savage' North American Indians. Charles Fox, with his immediate followers, supported him. Lord Derby, who was a follower of Fox in politics and had a long-standing social connection with him, said in his speech to the House of Lords on 16th November, 1778, that he now saw the impracticability of carrying on the war with America. [33, 34] Meanwhile, the French decided that the American rebels were a formidable force, and recognised their Declaration of Independence. They entered into an alliance with them, and declared war against Britain. Spain joined Britain's enemies in 1779, so that the Americans' independence was almost assured. [40]

John gradually withdrew more into his private life. Because he had failed to obtain an enquiry into his unlucky American venture, he wrote his own account of it in 1780. He devoted some of his time to his life-long love of art and drama, and, in the same year, he produced *The Lord of the Manor*, which was a comic opera in three parts. From 1782 until 1784 he held the position of Commander-in-Chief of the army in Ireland. [32]

A local legend about The Oaks alleged that the clumps of beech trees, which stood in the field on the opposite side of Woodmansterne Road at the south-eastern end of the parklands, were planted to commemorate the positions of the troops at Saratoga. However, it seems very unlikely that General Burgoyne wished to have a reminder of his defeat, or that his nephew, Lord Derby, had planted the trees for that purpose. In recent years, the old trees have been cut down and replaced by new ones.

Chapter 6

NEW SPORTING EVENTS AND
SOME THEATRICAL PURSUITS

The most successful years for Lord Derby on the turf were between 1778 and 1797. During the spring race-meeting on the downlands adjoining The Oaks in 1778, the Earl was entertaining a group of his sporting friends at the house for one week in May. The races that year were composed of heats run over two or four miles. Whilst they were dining after returning from the races, Lord Derby and his guests thought up one of the most famous events in the racing calendar when they decided to establish a new race on the Downs at Epsom in 1779. It would be for three-year-old fillies, and run over a distance of one and a half miles. Everyone agreed that it should be called the "Oaks" in honour of Lord Derby's sporting seat. It was an entirely new type of race, because, at this period in time, most races were run by more mature horses over a distance of at least two miles. [22]

There were seventeen subscribers at fifty guineas each for the first "Oaks" in 1779, and, appropriately, the race was won by Lord Derby's filly, *Bridget*. The event proved such a success that, later on the same day, when the Earl's guests returned to The Oaks, and dined there, they made another important decision while enjoying what Lord Rosebery called "Lord Derby's curious port". It was agreed to hold a new, short race for three-year-old colts and fillies over one straight mile at the meeting on the Downs at Epsom in 1780. [22] Sir Charles Bunbury, who was the first Steward of the Jockey Club when it was founded in 1750, was present on this occasion, and the Earl suggested that the new race should be called "The Bunbury". Sir Charles did not agree to this suggestion and, finally, the matter was settled allegedly on the "toss of a coin", and Lord Derby won. [51]

The first "Derby" was held on Epsom Downs on 4th May, 1780, and the meeting was enlivened by another of Lord Derby's favourite sports, cock-fighting. The "main of cocks" was between birds belonging to the gentlemen of Middlesex and Surrey. Meanwhile, nine out of the thirty-six horses entered for the race went to the starting post. The conditions for the event were "50 guineas - half forfeit", with a prize of one thousand and seventy-five guineas. Sir Charles Bunbury's horse, *Diomed*, ridden by Sam Arnull, was the first past the winning-post. [22] Lord Derby had to wait until 1787 before his *Sir Peter Teazle* won this most famous of all races for him. [36]

By 1784, the distance over which the Derby was run had been increased to one and a half miles. [22] The race-course had a "Captain Durand's Corner" between the starting-post and Tattenham Corner, and, adjacent to it, was "Durand's field". [52] The wealthy John Durand, who had made his fortune with the East India Company, both at sea and in

Bengal,[34] owned the Greyhound Inn at Carshalton, where horses entered for the races on the downlands could still be inspected, and cock-fighting was part of the entertainments there. [5] He also arranged the local field-sports, such as the hare-coursing on the downs, [53] and had gained quite a notoriety for his love of horse-racing and hunting. Therefore, it seems likely that he was included among Lord Derby's sporting friends, who had decided the arrangements for the Oaks and Derby races. In 1786, Mr. Durand became the Earl's neighbour, when he purchased Woodcote Lodge and Little Woodcote. [62] During the two years in which he lived here, he often entertained the sportsmen at his home, and a flag was flown on the roof of his house as a signal that he was ready to receive his guests.[53]

At the time of the first Oaks and Derby, Lord Derby's racing colours were green with a white stripe,and remained thus until 1787, when he changed them to black with a white cap, to avoid confusion with the colours of another owner. Since then, his family's racing colours have remained unchanged. In 1789, he won the Oaks for a second time with his filly, *Hermione*, but most of his horse-racing activities were centred at Newmarket, where the Jockey Club had its headquarters.[36]

Meanwhile, in about 1780, the opera singer, Susan Caulfield, became the mistress of Lord Derby's uncle, John Burgoyne, and, between the years 1782 and 1788, they had four children. [54] Their eldest child, John Fox Burgoyne, arrived on 24th July, 1782, and was destined to become a baronet in 1856, and a Field-Marshal in 1868, due to his successful army career, in which he distinguished himself in both the Peninsular and Crimean Wars. [36, 55]

Lord Derby's estranged wife, Betty, returned to London late in 1782, and, in the first instance, she went to live with her brother, the seventh Duke of Hamilton, in Portman Square. The Earl then gave her an allowance of £2,000 per annum which enabled her to live comfortably. Although she was not received by the Queen, she was welcomed back into society by her friends, who included the Prince of Wales. [36]

Meanwhile, Lord Derby enjoyed the congenial, male companionship he found at his clubs, at Newmarket, and at the cock-fights. His special political friends were Charles Fox and Edmund Burke. The politician and well-known wit of his time, George Selwyn commented on a discussion held at Brooks' Club in 1781, and said: "Lord Derby's nonsense is the only drawback upon the rest, he is the most méchant singe [naughty monkey] I ever knew." The Earl had gained favour in Walpole's opinion too, because on 10th July, 1782, he described the Whigs as: "without one speaker in the House of Lords but - Lord Derby".[56]

The Earl's own social circle included Richard Sheridan; the sculptress, Mrs. Damer; the actor and actress, Mr. and Mrs. Kemble; and Dr. Johnson's biographer, James Boswell.[56] During the 1780s, Lord Derby became involved with the amateur or "private theatricals" which were very fashionable at that time. Probably, his love of the theatre was due to John Burgoyne's influence, and, together with other ladies and gentlemen of high society, the

Edward 12th Earl of Derby, painted by George Romney.
A Private collection copyright reserved.

stage the plays, and coach the hosts and hostesses. Horace Walpole approved of these "theatricals" and commented on one play given at Richmond House that Lord Derby "delivered the 'charming prologue' most justly and admirably."[33]

It was through his involvement in these amateur theatrical productions that the Earl increased his friendship with the actress, Elizabeth (Eliza) Farren. [33] She was the daughter of George Farren, a surgeon and apothecary from Cork in Ireland, who had given up his medical career to become an actor. [55, 56] Miss Farren had learnt her stage-craft in the Manchester and Liverpool Theatres, before she made her first appearance on a London stage at the Haymarket Theatre on 9th June, 1777, where she played the part of Lady Hardcastle in Goldsmith's *She Stoops to Conquer*. Miss Farren's successful debut made her one of the most sought-after actresses to engage for other leading roles. [33]

In 1786, John Burgoyne wrote his most successful play, *The Heiress*, when he was staying at his nephew's family seat, Knowsley, and dedicated his work to Lord Derby. The Earl arranged for Elizabeth Farren to play the leading role in the London production of this comedy, [33] which became so popular that it was translated into several foreign languages. General Burgoyne's other works (apart from *The Maid of The Oaks*) were *Richard Coeur de Lion* and *The Lord of the Manor* (mentioned previously) - the latter being a conversion of Beaumont and Fletcher's *Custom of the Country*. [13, 54]

By 1787, the owner of The Oaks, William Lambert, had reached the age of twenty-six, and had married Jane Legrand of Guilton in Kent, who was a celebrated beauty of her time, and the unrivalled toast of her county. In 1788, William sold The Oaks to Lord Derby. The Earl also purchased one hundred and thirty-four acres of downs called "Oaks Down", or "Lambert's Oaks Down", with the adjoining fields, so that the whole of his estate then covered about one hundred and eighty-four acres. He enclosed a large area of the common fields to form a park around his house, and then added a plantation of trees about two miles in circumference on the outside of it. Two of the rights-of-way which ran across his estate were moved after he had obtained the consent of the Vestry of Woodmansterne. [9, 13] In 1775, Lancelot "Capability" Brown had been employed to make improvements to the grounds around Lord Derby's family seat at Knowsley. The main characteristics of a typical Brown landscape were isolated clumps of trees, "undulating greensward" and a surrounding belt of woodland [57]. Judging by these facts, it seems likely that Brown's designs influenced the Earl when he designed the landscape of his parklands around The Oaks, but, similar to other land-owners of that time, he would not live long enough to see all of his trees grow to maturity.

From the late eighteenth century onwards, the Earl was one of the most notable patrons of cock-fighting, and he became the champion of all England. He, and his father before him, had developed their own strain of cocks known as Black-breasted Reds, or the Knowsley Breed. It was said that, at one time, Lord Derby owned three thousand gamecocks, and his chief "feeder"(or breeder), who was called Potter, was famous throughout the country.

The Earl had his own pit in Preston, [36] and also had a cock-pit installed in his dining-room at The Oaks. The furniture would be cleared from the centre of this room, and sections of the floor were hinged back to reveal benches which unfolded from its underside around a square pit in the centre. [58]

Lord Derby's affection for Elizabeth Farren increased, and he openly sought her company as often as he could. There is no evidence that their friendship was more than a platonic one, but it did not escape the notice of the gossips, who spread some malicious rumours about them. [36] The Earl had called his colt which won the Derby in 1787, *Sir Peter Teazle*, because Miss Farren had played successfully the role of Lady Teazle in Sheridan's play, *The School for Scandal*. The Earl's filly, *Hermione*, which won the Oaks race in 1794, owed her name to Miss Farren's part as Queen Hermione in *The Winter's Tale* at the time of the filly's birth. [33]

Miss Farren had made her debut at Drury Lane on 8th September, 1788, in the role of Charlotte Rusper in *The West Indian*, and, from then onwards, she appeared at both this theatre and at the Haymarket Theatre, until she retired from the stage in 1797. Her successes included the parts of Lydia Languish, Millament, Lady Betty Modish, Merinthia in Sheridan's *Trip to Scarborough*, and Angelica in Congreve's *Love for Love*, [54,55] as well as Lady Teazle and Queen Hermione. Horace Walpole was one of her admirers, and to him, she was "the most perfect actress ever seen". William Hazlitt described her as: "Miss Farren, with her fine-lady airs and graces, with that elegant turn of the head and motion of her fan, and tripping of her tongue". Richard Cumberland thought her style was "exquisite". [32] Her natural dignity and "ease of manner" had enabled her to receive many invitations to join the London society in their dinners, parties and entertainments. [33] Before she had become friendly with Lord Derby, she had a short affair with John Palmer, and was admired by Charles Fox. [32] Her portrait was painted by Sir Thomas Lawrence. [55]

By 1791, Lord Derby was spending more of his time with Elizabeth Farren, [56] who lived in Green Street, Grosvenor Square, [36] in the most fashionable part of London, and not far from the Earl's town-house. Horace Walpole commented that he was constantly meeting "Lord Derby and the Farrens". In a letter dated 19th September, 1793, he wrote: "In the evening, we went together to Miss Farren's, and besides her duenna-mother, found her at piquet with her unalterable Earl. Apropos, I have observed of late years, that when Earls take strong attachment, they are more steady than other men."[56]

Within his own family circle, the Earl had suffered a sad loss when his uncle, John Burgoyne, died suddenly at his home in Hertford Street, Mayfair, on 3rd June, 1792. He was buried in the cloisters of Westminster Abbey. [13] Lord Derby became the guardian of his uncle's four children by Susan Caulfield, and brought them up. He sent the eldest boy, John Fox Burgoyne, to Eton and Woolwich for a good education, and launched him on his army career at the age of sixteen. [36] The Earl's own son and heir, Lord Edward Smith Stanley, graduated from Cambridge in 1795, and, in the following year, he became the Member of Parliament for Preston, as a supporter of the Whig Party, although he made little impression on the affairs of the Commons. [32]

The youngest of Lord Derby's daughters, Elizabeth Henrietta, married Stephen Cole of Twickenham in 1795, and became known as Lady Elizabeth Cole. The Earl's eldest daughter's wedding took place in 1796, and Charlotte's bridegroom was her cousin, Edmund Hornby, the son of the Earl's sister, the Honourable Lucy, and her husband, the Reverend Geoffrey Hornby of Dalston Hall in Westmoreland. [32, 36] The girl's mother, Betty, the Countess of Derby, now suffered from tuberculosis, from which she died at the age of forty-four years, on 14th March, 1797, at her home in Gloucester Street, Marylebone. [36]

The Earl did not grieve over his wife's death, and planned to marry Miss Farren just a few weeks later. [36] She made her last appearance on the stage on 8th April, 1797, when she played Lady Teazle, and attracted a large audience. After speaking her final lines, she burst into tears, and then her co-actor, Wroughton, recited some not very brilliant lines of farewell. [32] Her marriage to Lord Derby took place at his town-house in Grosvenor Square on Monday, 2nd May, 1797. They were married by special licence, and the Earl's brother-in-law, the Reverend Geoffrey Hornby, who was then the vicar of Winwick in Lancashire, performed the ceremony. Afterwards, the wedding party went to St James's Palace, where Queen Charlotte gave a reception in honour of the bride. On that day, the Earl entered the happiest period of his long life. At last, he had a devoted wife, whom he, in turn, adored.[36]

Chapter 7   THE IDYLLIC YEARS

A description of Lord Derby's hunting and racing seat at The Oaks in 1798 was given by the Reverend William Gilpin senior M.A., (formerly headmaster of Cheam School, and devotee of the picturesque in landscape) in his *Observations on the Western Parts of England*, which was published in that year. He described the house in these terms: "Though the little villa is whimsical and singular, it has its beauty. It commands about twenty acres, in an oblong form. In the centre stands the house, which is a kind of tower, but yet unfinished. One half of the ground is laid out in close walks winding among oaks, from whence the place has its name; the other is a hanging lawn, interspersed with fir, flowering shrubs and beeches. ... The whole is surrounded by a sunk fence; and like an inchanted (sic) island in a desert, appears a beautiful spot from every part of the Downs in its neighbourhood, and has itself a grand view over them, as far as the towers of London." [59]   From the Reverend Mr. Gilpin's comments, the landscape here appeared to be different then, in comparison to the present-day scenery.

Lord Derby was forty-four years old, and his second Countess was thirty-nine when they married. Between 1797 and 1801, they had four children, but only one of them survived to adulthood. Their first child was still-born on 27th March, 1798; their second, Lucy Elizabeth, arrived on 12th March, 1799, and died at the age of ten. James Smith Stanley was born on 9th March, 1800, and lived until he was seventeen years old. He was followed by Mary Margaret on 3rd March 1801, and, eventually, she became the wife of Thomas Egerton, the second Earl of Wilton, and her death occurred in 1860.

Soon after his father's marriage, Lord Derby's heir, Lord Edward Smith Stanley, had married his cousin, Charlotte Margaret Hornby, who was one of the daughters of the Earl's sister, the Honourable Lucy, and her husband, the Reverend Geoffrey Hornby. Their son, another Edward, was born on 19th March, 1799. [32] Thus, by 1803, the Earl and his wife were surrounded by the youngest members of their family, because there were four Stanley children and grandchildren under four years of age, as well as the four young Burgoynes, who were in the care of Lord Derby. They gave their deepest affection to the Earl, and received the same from him throughout his life. He and his wife spent most of their time at Knowsley, and the Countess presided over their lively household, which increased in numbers when other relatives, mostly the Hornbys, came to stay, and remained there for many weeks. [33]   However, the Earl continued to enjoy all of his sporting activities, and he regularly attended the race-meetings at Epsom and elsewhere. [36]

After the Prince of Wales had visited Knowsley in 1806, the Earl decided to extend his home to accommodate his many visitors and their servants. He and his wife then spent the following winter and spring at The Oaks and Grosvenor Square while the additions and alterations were carried out. [33] Lord Derby already had a pack of stag-hounds at The Oaks, and some stags were brought here from Knowsley Park at the beginning of the

Elizabeth (Eliza) Farren, second wife of the 12th Earl of Derby. Copied from an original portrait by Thomas Lawrence. A Private collection, copyright reserved

nineteenth century, [60] and were kept in his deer paddock situated by the lane leading to the village of Woodmansterne. [61] His hounds earned a high reputation among his hunting friends, some of whom came from London to hunt with him. [60] It was alleged that, on one occasion, they rode as far as Tunbridge Wells before the kill. [50] Among the local huntsmen was the Earl's neighbour, the rich young Mr. John Hodsdon Durand, who lived at Woodcote Lodge (now Woodcote Hall). He had inherited the Little Woodcote Estate and the Greyhound Inn at Carshalton on his father's death in July 1788, and had taken over Mr. Durand senior's place in Lord Derby's circle of sportsmen. As a keen supporter of horse-racing, he had tried to win the Derby on Epsom Downs, but his colt by *Saltram* was listed as an "also ran" in 1795, and so was his *Sheet Anchor* in 1798. [62] He also organised the annual field-sports, including hare-coursing, on the downlands in February, March, October and November. [53]

Stag-hunting with the Earl gave Mr. Durand so much pleasure that he erected a wooden tower, with an interior staircase leading up to a large metal and gilt stag on the top of it, on the site of the Late Bronze Age enclosure on the hill top opposite The Oaks, so that it could be seen from the windows on the north side of the house. It commemorated those happy days spent with Lord Derby's staghounds, and the land around this "monument" became known as "Stag Field". Although this structure was removed long before the end of the nineteenth century, the field's name lasted until it was incorporated into the southern end of the grounds of Queen Mary's Hospital early this century. [63, 64] When the Earl gave up his stag-hunting, his hounds became a subscription pack under the name of "The Surrey Staghounds" and were kept in kennels at Horley in Surrey. [60]

In 1809, the Reverend Owen Manning and William Bray published the second volume of their *History and Antiquities of the County of Surrey*, in which they mentioned a very large old beech tree in the grounds of The Oaks at that time. It had a trunk of twenty-five and a half feet in circumference, and its branches grew into each other, and were, allegedly, hollow. The villagers of Woodmansterne believed that there was a spring of water in it, but, possibly, this story arose from the fact that plenty of rainwater was collected in it. Beneath the tree stood the stone which John Lambert had placed there in 1501. [8]

At the end of 1814, The Oaks became the scene of preparations for a wedding; although, on this occasion, there was no expensive Fête Champêtre. Miss Maria Sophie Burgoyne, a daughter of the late General, and cousin and ward of Lord Derby, had lived here for some years at the beginning of the nineteenth century. As a result, one of the most notable weddings held at St. Peter's Church in Woodmansterne took place on 22nd December, 1814, when Miss Burgoyne married the Earl's nephew, Phipps Hornby. The Earl and his son, Lord Edward Stanley, signed the register as witnesses to the ceremony. [65] The bridegroom was the fifth son of Lord Derby's sister, Lucy, and the Reverend Geoffrey Hornby. [32]

Phipps Hornby was twenty-nine years old at the time of his marriage, and already had experienced a distinguished naval career. He entered the navy in May, 1797, and served under Captain Bligh (of the mutiny on the Bounty fame). After service off the coast of North America and in the West Indies, he joined Nelson's ship, the *Victory*, in 1804. Nelson promoted him to be lieutenant of the *Excellent*. He remained in the Mediterranean until 1816, was wounded and saw plenty of action during the Napoleonic war with France. He was promoted to Captain and after the "brilliant frigate action of Lissa", together with the other captains, was rewarded with a gold medal in March, 1811. After his marriage, he returned to sea, and received the Austrian Order of St. Joseph of Wurtemburg for co-operating with the Tuscan troops in taking Elba from the French. On 4th June, 1815, he was nominated as a Companion of the Order of the Bath. He withdrew from active service in the summer of 1816, but resumed his naval career in 1832, and, before his death in March, 1867, he rose to the rank of Admiral, having received his honours as Knight Commander of the Order of the Bath in April, 1852, and Knight Grand Cross of the same Order in June, 1861. He and his wife had several daughters and two sons. Their eldest boy was destined to become Sir Geoffrey Thomas Phipps Hornby, and was made an Admiral of the Fleet in 1891, while the younger became the Reverend James John Hornby, D.D., and was the Provost of Eton. [32, 55]

Lord Derby entertained some notable guests at The Oaks during the Regency period, and, allegedly, had more than fifty bedrooms here in which to accommodate them. [39] The Prince Regent was a frequent guest in the racing seasons, although he had not won the Derby with any of his race-horses since he was the Prince of Wales, when his horse, *Sir Thomas*, was the winner in 1788 [36]. Other members of the Royal Family stayed here, and so did the Forresters, the Ansons and the Bentincks, together with some of the leading sportsmen and politicians of that time. [66]

The Oaks also attracted several artists during the earlier years of the nineteenth century. James Barenger junior, (1780-1831) painted *Lord Derby's Fox-hounds* in 1809, and his painting of '*Darling,' a Staghound at Earl of Derby's Park* was exhibited at the Royal Academy in 1818. In Barenger's *The Earl of Derby's Staghounds* (1823)) two of the huntsmen are Lord Edward Stanley and the Honourable Edward: the Earl's son and grandson. The scene depicts the downlands near The Oaks (Banstead Downs) with the Banstead Windmill in the background, on the site of which Banstead Hospital was built later in that century. Another artist, Henry William Burgess (1792-1844) painted *A study of an old beech tree at The Oakes* [sic], *Surrey, the seat of the Earl of Derby,* which was exhibited at the Royal Academy in 1815. [67] It has been alleged that John Constable's *The White Horse* was painted at The Oaks in 1819, [51] and showed the house in the background to the smithy. Constable visited Shortes Place in Woodmansterne, where he stayed with the now aging William Lambert and his second wife with the unusual name of Nutty. In January, 1825, he painted their three grandchildren while they were staying with their grandparents. *The Lambert Children* shows Mary sitting on a donkey, and her brothers, William and George Patrick, standing on either side of her in front of Woodmansterne Church. Constable's portrait of their grandfather was painted in the same year. [11] John Hassell, the artist and author of *Picturesque Rides and Walks within Thirty Miles of the British Metropolis* (1817-1818) which he illustrated himself, gave a short history of The Oaks in his book. He states that the Earl " has added, at the west end, a large brick building with four turrets at each corner". Hassell adds: "The palace [sic] grounds are spacious and abound in noble timber ... There are upwards of fifty bedrooms accommodating sportsmen or guests to his Lordship, who, it has been observed before, has a pack of Stag-hounds in his establishment". [53]

Probably, the only disappointment for the Earl at this time was the fact that his son and heir, Lord Edward, had not inherited an interest in horse-racing and other sports. Instead, he became very interested in zoology, and set up a private menagerie at Knowsley, costing between £10,000 and £15,000 to maintain each year. It occupied one hundred acres of land, and seventy acres of water, and his agent collected specimens for the zoo from all over the world. Lord Edward gave his own daily care to his collection, making copious notes and observations on it. [32]

Lord Edward and his wife, Charlotte, had three sons and four daughters. Their eldest son, Edward George Geoffrey Smith Stanley, made up for his father's lack of interest in sporting activities, and had a life-long passionate devotion to sports, including shooting and racing. In his boyhood, portraits of him were painted by George Romney and Sir Thomas Lawrence. He was educated at Oxford and began training race-horses when he was young. He then managed his grandfather's racing stud, but he never won the Derby, Oaks or St. Leger races. He did have some successes with his horses in other races and, when he ended his career on the turf after twenty-two years, he had gained £94,000 in stakes alone. The eminent nineteenth-century diarist, Charles Greville, who was another horse-racing enthusiast, knew young Edward well - but neither liked nor trusted him. In his diary, he described Edward's boisterousness, undignified manners, and sharp practices on the race-courses. [32]

However, young Edward pleased his grandfather with his political, as well as his racing, career. He had far more success in Parliament than his father achieved, and was destined to become Prime Minister three times, later in the nineteenth century. After he left Oxford University, he entered the House of Commons on 6th March, 1820, as the Member for Stockbridge and a supporter of the Whig Party. His step-grandmother had given him elocution lessons, [36] which, undoubtedly, enabled him to make his successful maiden speech on 30th March, 1824, and then he proved himself to be a powerful debater. [32] Lord Derby, who was a very shrewd and sagacious man, would question his grandson's successes in most of his political triumphs, despite his merits. [69] In the autumn of 1824, Edward travelled to Canada and the United States. On his return, he married Emma Caroline, the second daughter of Edward Bootle-Wilbraham, (later Lord Skelmersdale) in May, 1825, and their eldest son, Edward Henry Stanley, was born on 31st July, 1826. [32]

The Earl's happiest years came to an end when Elizabeth, the second Countess of Derby, died on 23rd April, 1829. Their daughter, Lady Margaret, who was now the Countess of

The ... k ... b 1920 L C E Press ...

Wilton, went to Knowsley to preside over her father's household. Lord Derby was sustained by his interest in his grandson's political career. Edward had been re-elected, this time as the Member for Preston, in June, 1826. [32] and became the Under-Secretary for the Colonies in 1827 and 1828. He was the Chief Secretary for Ireland from 1830 to 1833, by which time he was described in Charles Greville's diary as an orator and statesman, "only second, if second, to Peel", but also had thoughts "only for the turf, and an interest in the lottery".[68]

Although the second Countess of Derby's death was mourned by all members of her family and friends, regardless of their age, none missed her more than the old Earl did, after over thirty-two years of a very happy marriage. However, he did not withdraw from public life, and maintained his interest in his sporting activities. [33] The social gatherings continued at The Oaks during the races held on Epsom Downs, but, in 1833, that year's party was given by Lord Derby's grandson. Charles Greville was invited there on 27th May, 1833, during his week at Epsom for the races, and noted in his diary that "Stanley kept house for the first and probably (for the house is for sale) for the last time." Greville had entered one of his horses for the Derby, "but was beat easily, my horse not being good".[69]

Charles Greville was a well-known personality on the turf, and a member of the Jockey Club. From 1821 to 1826, he had managed the stables of the Duke of York, who was his great friend. At the time of his visit to The Oaks, he was in partnership with his cousin, Lord George Bentinck, and trained race-horses. He was known by his nick-name of "Punch", but also was called "Gruncher" behind his back, due to his sombre manner. [32, 54]

In his description of his visit to The Oaks, Greville described it as: "a very agreeable place, with an odd sort of house built at different times and by different people; but the outside is covered with ivy and creepers, which is pretty, and there are two good living-rooms in it. Besides this, there is an abundance of grass and shade; it has been for thirty or forty years the resort of all our old Jockeys, and is wound up by the sporting portion of the Government." The other visitors on that day included Lord Grey and his daughter, the Duke and Duchess of Richmond, Lord and Lady Errol, Lord Althorp, "Graham, Uxbridge, Charles Grey [the second son of Earl Grey] the Duke of Grafton, Lichfield and Stanley"s brothers." The entertainments for the guests were: "racing all the morning, an excellent dinner, and whist and blind hookey in the evening." [69]

At the beginning of 1834, a new owner took over The Oaks, when Sir Charles Edward Grey of Portman Square in London , bought the house and its estate from Lord Derby on 8th February, for the sum of £9,100. A Lieutenant-Colonel John Grey of Brighton, a likely relative, and , probably, Sir Charles's brother, was involved as well in this transaction. [70] Thus, Lord Edward Stanley and his sporting friends had to look elsewhere for their social gatherings during the race-meetings on Epsom Downs. Barrow Hedges also was no longer available to the sportsmen. The house had been sold after the Scawen estates went into receivership in 1779, and, from the beginning of the nineteenth century it became a non-sporting private residence. [27, 52]

Lord Derby lived only for another eight months after the sale of The Oaks. His death occurred on 21st October, 1834, and he was buried next to his second Countess in Ormskirk Church. He had been the Earl of Derby for fifty-eight years, and had maintained his interest in horse-racing and cock-fighting up to the last days of his life. It was alleged that a cock-fight took place on his bedroom floor when he lay on his death bed. He had seen the beginning of the industrial revolution, and the new method of travel by rail during the latter years of his life, when, perhaps, his two main regrets had been his son's and grandson's political change of allegiance from the Whig Party to the Tory government in 1824, and young Lord Edward's defeat by Henry Hunt in the Preston by-election of December 1830. [33]

Chapter 8

A DESIRABLE COUNTRY RESIDENCE

Before Sir Charles Edward Grey bought The Oaks, he had returned to England from India, where he had been the Chief Justice of Calcutta in Bengal. Born in 1785, he was the younger son of Mr. R. W. Grey of Backworth in Northumberland, who had once held the position of High Sheriff. Sir Charles had been educated at University College, Oxford, and had graduated in 1806. After winning an English Essay Prize, he was elected Fellow of Oriel College. He was called to the Bar in 1811, and, in 1817, was appointed as a Commissioner in Bankruptcy. His involvement in Indian affairs began in 1820, when he became a Judge in the Supreme Court of Madras, and received his knighthood with his appointment. [32]

In 1821, Sir Charles married Miss Elizabeth Jervoise, who was one of the daughters of the Reverend Sir Samuel Jervoise, Bart., and his wife, Lady Elizabeth, of Isleworth Park in Horndean, Hampshire. [71] The newly-weds returned to India and lived in Madras until 1825, when Sir Charles was transferred to the Supreme Court of Bengal, and took up his appointment as Chief Justice in Calcutta. [32] On their return to England, they moved into a house in Portman Square, London. [70]

Sir Charles had just over one year in which to enjoy life at his country residence, The Oaks, and to take part in the sporting activities on the adjoining downlands, before he became involved, once again, in colonial affairs. By the end of June, 1835, he had been appointed as one of three Commissioners (the others were Lord Gosford and Sir George Gipps) who were sent to Canada to enquire into the causes of discontent there. [32] Before setting out on his journey, he went to the Court of St. James on 1st July, 1835, to be sworn in as a Privy Councillor, together with Lord Charles Fitzroy, who was the Member of Parliament for Bury St. Edmunds, and a second son of the fourth Duke of Grafton. [72]

Charles Greville, who was Clerk to the Privy Council, was present when Sir Charles was sworn in as a Privy Councillor, and recorded in his diary that a unique incident took place after the ceremony was over. King William IV, who was not famous for eloquent speeches, astounded everyone, including his ministers, by addressing a fairly long speech to Sir Charles, in which His Majesty reminded him that he was about to embark on one of the most important missions sent to Canada. The King also told him that he must remember that the colony was not peopled from "the Mother Country" like other colonies. It was not, originally, a possession of the Crown, but had been obtained "by the sword". Care should be taken to assert the undoubted prerogative of the Crown, which the King was determined to "enforce and maintain", and of which, he said, "persons, who ought to have known better, have dared, even in my presence, to deny the existence". [72]

A stunned silence followed this outburst of eloquence. The King's astonished minister: were not sure to whom the latter remark referred! However, the mystery was solved two weeks later, after Melbourne remonstrated with the King over his speech to Sir Charle: Grey. His Majesty explained that he had been irritated by a remark made to him by Lord Glenelg, who had contradicted him in a discussion about the old constitution of Canada Although William IV made "a sort of apology" to Glenelg, the royal bitterness was no diminished on that subject. [72]

Sir Charles returned from Canada in November, 1836, leaving his two colleagues there The results of his inquiries into the colony's troubles must have satisfied the King and hi ministers, because he received the reward of the Grand Cross of Hanover, and became a Knight Commander of the Hanoverian Guelphic Order (K.C.H.). He then tried to ente Parliament in 1837 as the Member for Tynemouth, but lost the election. He had mor success in the following year, when his opponent there, Sir G.F. Young, was unseated on petition. He then supported the Whig administration from 1838 until its dissolution in 1841. [32]

The diarist, Charles Greville, knew Sir Charles Grey well, and described him as: "thoug ridiculous-looking, not at all a stupid man". Greville recorded that Sir Charles wa commonly known as "Mr. Pickwick", and usually wore a brown coat. He also had reputation for his wit, and was a member of the "The Club" [73], which was founded b Dr. Johnson in 1764, and later known as "The Literary Club".

After his term of office as the Member of Parliament of Tynemouth ended in 1841, Si Charles was appointed as the Governor of Barbados, St. Vincent, Tobago, Trinidad an St. Louis, and held this office until 1846. He was very popular during his appointment a the Governor of Jamaica from 1847 until 1853, but his wife, Lady Elizabeth, died there i 1850.[32] Meanwhile, because of his involvement in colonial affairs, and his absence from England, he had already sold The Oaks to a Mr. Joseph Smith on 25th December, 1842.[7]

Joseph Smith was forty-one years old when he purchased The Oaks, having been born i Coventry in 1801. His wife, Augusta, (née Gilliat), began her life in Islington in 180(and was probably related to him, as his mother's name had been Gilliat before he marriage. His sister, Emma, who was born in 1809, had married a John Jones. [11] At th beginning of Mr. Smith's ownership of The Oaks, the house was converted into tw residences "without the slightest degree injuring its effect, either en masse or in detail", [7] so that it also could provide Joseph's sister and brother-in-law with a home.

By the time Mr. and Mrs. Smith moved to The Oaks, they already had an only child Frederick, who was ten years old. Mr. and Mrs. Jones had a daughter, another Emm aged eight. She was followed by Mary and John Algernon, both arriving in 1845, an then there were three more sons before Mrs. Jones's death occurred in late July, 184 when she was thirty-nine years old. She was buried at Woodmansterne on 2nd Augus

1848. Afterwards, John Jones left The Oaks and went to live in Wales, where he became a farmer. After he died in 1876 in Merioneth (now Clwyd) at the age of seventy-eight, his body was returned to Woodmansterne and his funeral took place on 6th December, 1876. The memorial on his grave, surrounded by railings, is the largest in the churchyard. [11, 65]

At The Oaks, Joseph Smith had enlarged his estate when he bought some more land for the Oaks Farm from William Lambert on 23rd March, 1849. [76] He then became Lord of the Manor of Woodmansterne, which he purchased, together with the manor house and seventy acres of land, from the Reverend John George Stovie, who was the vicar of Camberwell. [13] Mr. Smith also became a Justice of the Peace. [11]

At some time (date unknown) after John Jones's departure from The Oaks, a fire severely damaged the middle block of it. Joseph Smith, with his unknown architect, rebuilt the centre portion of the house to a lower elevation than the original one, and made other alterations to a design based on Robert Adam's castle style, also taking the opportunity to "regularise" the appearance of the building. Probably, he added the projecting, two-storey bay and Venetian window by the middle of the north (rear) side, as well as the wide, canted bays here at each end, both of which rose as irregular, octagonal towers. These features do not appear on the designs for The Oaks made by Robert Adam. [31]

Apparently, Mr. Smith "spared no expense in placing The Oaks in a state of complete repair", [75] and, allegedly, he made some "very considerable interior alterations" to the house, which was "greatly improved". [13] A comparison of the etching dated 1819 with the later photographs of The Oaks, shows the replacement of the four-storey centre portion attributed to Sir Robert Taylor by one of a much lower elevation, thus reducing the number of rooms here.

By 1856, Joseph Smith's household had been enlarged again, after his nephew, Frederick Gilliat Smith, with his wife, Jessie Annette, moved into The Oaks to live with their uncle and aunt. [11] Their family increased with the births of their five children, who were baptised at St. Peter's Church in Woodmansterne. They were Alice Augusta on 13th February, 1856; Frederick Ernest Gilliat on 5th September, 1856; Harold Gilliat on 9th May, 1861; Jessie Lilian Gilliat on 12th April, 1863; and Mabel Rose Gilliat on 22nd April, 1868. [65] Their father also took an active part in the affairs of the church, and he was a churchwarden at St. Peter's from 1857 to 1859. [11]

Joseph and Augusta Smith became grandparents after their son, Frederick, married, and he and his wife, Alice, had two children, whose births occurred in 1859 and 1861 respectively. At The Oaks, Mr. Smith's nephew and his young family were still in residence here during the early 1870s. [11] A large conservatory was erected in the grounds on the western side of the house, and provided more heated facilities for growing exotic plants and ferns than the two smaller greenhouses at the rear of it. [77]

By 1873, Mr. Smith had made a decision to sell The Oaks, and it was put on the market.

Part of the sale catalogue is still in existence, and describes some of the domestic quarters of the house, as well as the outbuildings and grounds. The scullery had an "Eagle" range measuring four feet six inches, an enamelled sink with hot and cold water, and shelves. The larder was paved with tiles and its walls were lined to the ceiling with white tiles, similar to the well-ventilated dairy, with its slate shelves and fountain in the centre of it, for cooling purposes. There was a game larder, and a wash-house with a baking-oven, sink and a large copper in it; also a china pantry and knife-house, each fitted with shelves, a lamp room, water closet and a boot house. On the basement floor, there were four large cellars, and a small one, with paved floors, and two of these were fitted with wine bins. Outside was a coal-yard and coal-cellar for indoor use. [77]

At that time, the outbuildings included a detached, brick-built building, which was used as the male servants' living and sleeping rooms. It had a water closet, and a small bedroom with a separate entrance. Two more water closets, which had been built recently, were fitted with "Jennings's apparatus", and there was a large tank for water storage; and a well, which was three hundred feet in depth. The stabling consisted of a four-stall stable, four loose-boxes, and the harness, saddle and coachman's rooms. There was a large, double coach-house with a loft, a single coach-house, a paved yard and a manure pit. [77]

Near to the house stood the newly-erected conservatory, which was divided into five compartments (this is now called "The Grotto") and, behind it, were the toilet facilities for the gardeners, a mushroom house, fruit house, potting shed, seed room, a boiler house with a drying room over it, an open shed and a carpenter's shop. The vinery here was fifty-one feet in length, with a tool-house at the rear of it; also two small greenhouses heated by hot water pipes, and two soft-water tanks with a pump. The walled kitchen garden opposite the Oaks Farm was about one and a half acres in size, and contained a large peach house eighty-eight feet in length, as well as the thirty-foot long plant house forcing frames, etc., choice fruit trees and a high-pressure water supply. [77]

On the opposite side of the lane (now Croydon Lane) stood the farm buildings, which were comprised of a roofed-in entrance gateway, the bailiff's house with seven rooms, a dairy, the carter's cottage with five rooms, an open cart shed with a granary over it, a two-stalled stable with a loose-box, a poultry house, a cow house for five cows, a calf pen, a meal house with a copper, and a root house. There was also an open shed around the farmyard, some piggeries, a barn with a tiled roof, a lambing shed, a large implement shed and another shed, which had been erected recently. The chaff-cutting room had a small steam engine and gear, as well as a saw table with a circular saw. In addition, a four-roomed cottage and garden stood adjacent to the farm buildings and a blacksmith's shop was sited opposite to it. The sale catalogue stated that "this small portion of the property is let off", and provided the information that the Sutton Water Company's water already supplied both The Oaks and its farm by that time. [77]

The pleasure gardens near the house had spacious, well-kept lawns, and was well timbered with old oak, beech, lime and other trees and shrubs. The flower garden here

General John Burgoyne, son-in-law of the 11th Earl of Derby, painted by Sir Joshua Reynolds.
© *the Frick Collection, New York.*

The ladies' cricket match at The Oaks in 1777, played by the Countess of Derby and friends, From a watercolour by 'T.H.' dated 1779.
© *Marylebone Cricket Club.*

Barrow Hedges, 1825. From a painting by Gideon Yates.

The Earl of Derby's staghounds. From a painting by James Barenger. The background is presumably Banstead Downs, with Banstead windmill (site of Banstead Hospital) on the horizon. The huntsmen include Lord Stanley and the Hon. Edward Stanley.

contained the "rosery" and shrubberies. Beyond the lawns were the timbered park and pasture lands, with a newly-erected gamekeeper's house and outbuildings, which included the pheasantry, fowl houses and runs. [77] These buildings stood on the site of the present-day copse used in recent years as a camping ground for Scouts and Guides.

Despite all of these essential amenities for a country gentleman's estate, The Oaks remained on the market for another four years, during which time, Frederick Gilliat Smith bought some land from his uncle on 10th May, 1876. [76] Joseph Smith died towards the end of that year, at the age of seventy-eight, and was buried at Woodmansterne on 6th December, 1876. [65] Afterwards, his nephew was involved in the sale of the house, the Oaks Farm and the estate, and on 25th July, 1877, Mr. Daniel Aldersley Taylor became the new owner of them. [76]

Born on 12th September, 1819, Daniel Aldersley Taylor was the eldest son of Daniel Taylor the younger, and his wife, Sophia (née Stephens Aldersley) of Church Row in Bromley, Kent. When he grew up, Daniel junior went into the family business of Daniel Taylor & Sons, Wine and Brandy Merchants. On 24th July, 1845, he had married Louisa Morecroft, who was the daughter of Mr. Thomas Morecroft, a solicitor of Liverpool and Higher Baldington in Cheshire. [58] They had one son, Daniel Maynard Taylor, and three daughters, Elizabeth Johnston, Sophia Louisa, and Kate Morecroft. [78]

By the time he moved to The Oaks, Mr. Taylor was an experienced man on the turf. He kept his horses here, and some of them were entered for the races. During his period of residence, a large house-party for the Derby and the Oaks was held at the house each year. For the latter race, all of the men wore sprays of oak leaves in the buttonholes of their morning coats, instead of the conventional carnations from the hothouse. [58] In 1880, Mr. Taylor's racing colours for the flat season were registered as a white jacket and blue cap. [79]

Among Mr. Aldersley Taylor's possessions at The Oaks were a Chinese Chippendale table; a Dresden clock; one satinwood bookcase with two shelves; a pair of parquetry cupboards with shelves; as well as a low chair which was included in a picture of his wife, Louisa. He owned portraits of his grandfather, Daniel Taylor, and a pastel of William Aldersley. His great-grandson, the late Mr. A. Maynard-Taylor, inherited these portraits; the large, leather-bound bible used daily for morning prayers at The Oaks; and a framed, sequin fan belonging to his great-aunt, Kate Morecroft Caldbeck (née Taylor). The last ball given by her father was held at the house in her honour. The cock-pit installed in the ground-floor room here by the twelfth Earl of Derby was still in existence at that time, and the floor could be hinged back to reveal benches on the underside of it around a square pit in the centre. [58]

In 1880, Mr. Taylor's son, Daniel, moved to a house in Banstead. [58] Later, he bought Heath House (in Sutton Lane) in 1913, where he resided until his death in October, 1926. Part of his residence became the Greenacres School for Girls, and the old coach-house

The Taylor family bible, used daily for morning prayers at The Oaks 1877 - 1884.

and stables were converted into a house for the headmistress. [79, 80] Meanwhile, his father at The Oaks had died on 2nd April, 1884. [81] His will shows that he also owned properties in Chester, "and elsewhere in the United Kingdom", in New Zealand and, possibly, in his words, in "any other of Her Majesty's colonies or dependencies". Among his bequests, he left the residue of his personal estate, including his farming stock in New Zealand, to the use of his wife, Louisa, and his son-in-law, the Reverend William Baker, who was married to his eldest daughter, Kate Morecroft. [78]

After Mr. Taylor's death, his widow, Louisa, decided to sell The Oaks, and Mr. Richard Higgins bought the house and its estate from her and her late husband's executors on 1st October, 1884. [76] Mrs. Taylor then moved to a residence in Stanhope Gardens in South Kensington, which she owned until her death. Both Mr. and Mrs. Taylor were buried in the family's vault at West Norwood. [79]

When Mr. Higgins bought The Oaks in 1884, the estate then contained just over one hundred and eighty acres of land. He also owned other lands in the area, including some pastures on the east side of the present-day Medical Research Council's Laboratories, and these fields have been covered by houses in the present century. [81] He kept The Oaks in his possession for a further four years until 1st October, 1888, when he sold it, together with its estate and the Oaks Farm, to Mr. Harry Berkeley James of Ashburn Place, South Kensington, for the sum of £22,500.[76] Mr. and Mrs. James were very friendly with Mr. Daniel Maynard-Taylor at Banstead, and it seems likely that their friendship with him prompted them to move to the locality. They were the last people to use The Oaks as a private residence. [81]

Henry Berkeley James, (usually known as Harry), was born in Walsall in 1846, and married his wife, Lucy, there in 1880. [11] He had a unique collection of South American birds, which were kept at The Oaks. [9] Mr James became churchwarden of St. Peter's Church in Woodmansterne in 1890, and, in the same year, his son, Adrian Ingham, was baptised here. [11, 65] After Mr. James's death on 22nd July, 1892, [82] when he was about forty-six years of age, a plaque to his memory was installed in the church. [11]

Lucy James and her family continued to live at The Oaks after her husband's death, and she took part in the affairs of Woodmansterne. She was a churchwarden as well as a parish councillor during the years 1896 to 1905. [11] In 1897, she was hostess to some members of the Surrey Archaeological Society, whose annual excursion was held on Wednesday, 28th July, when The Oaks was among the places which they visited. They inspected the "beautiful modern drawing-room" by courtesy of Mrs. James and Mr. Ralph Nevill, F.S.A., who was a member of the party, related a brief history of the house. On leaving there, they were entertained by Mr. F. Lambert at Garratt's Hall in Banstead, which had historical connections with the old Lambert's Oaks. They were able to inspect the fireplace with the date "1584" over it, as well as the early seventeenth-century fire dogs of Dutch workmanship - all of which had been removed from Shortes Place in Woodmansterne. [16]

The Oaks in 1888. Note the middle front section rebuilt after the fire in the 1840s.

During the nineteenth century, reforms had taken place in the system of local government, which had not been, in the modern sense, representative, because the powers of administration were exercised by certain men only, resident in a locality, and through the Parish Council. Elected representatives were introduced into the boroughs in 1834, and the counties in 1888 (with limited franchise). In 1894 came the creation of Urban and Rural District Councils elected under a wider, but still not universal, franchise. The old parish boundary between Woodmansterne and Carshalton was altered, and The Oaks, its estate and farm, became part of the area covered by the new Carshalton Urban District Council. [5]

At the beginning of the present century, part of the late Mr. James's unique collection of birds was displayed in the South Kensington Museum, but many of the beautiful specimens remained at The Oaks. [9] On 30th August, 1911, another wedding was celebrated at the house, when Lucy James's daughter, Inez Mary, married John Murray at St. Peter's Church in Woodmansterne. The bride was twenty-seven years old, and the bridegroom, aged twenty-eight, was a civil engineer of Banstead, and the son of Malcolm Brown Murray, who was a distiller. The Dean of Ossory, the Reverend T. E. Winder, performed the ceremony, which was witnessed by the bride's mother, and Charlotte Jane Murray and Nevisa Clarke. [83]

In 1912, Mrs. James had decided to sell The Oaks and its estate. It is one of the houses of historical interest for which complete sales catalogues remain to give precise, detailed descriptions of the properties before their decline, alteration, or total demolition. Therefore, from the brochure of July, 1912, it is possible to ascertain the exact size and number of rooms in the house, its outbuildings, and details of the grounds, the estate and the Oaks Farm at that time (see Appendix I). Also, two photographs showing the front and rear of the house are enclosed with the brochure. [84]

The Oaks was put up for sale by auction on 16th July, 1912, "at 2 p.m. precisely", at The Mart, Tokenhouse Yard, in London. The auctioneers were Messrs. Walton & Lee of 10, Mount Street, Grosvenor Square, and the estate agents were Messrs. Robert M. Fuller, Moon & Fuller, of 83, High Street, Croydon. Apart from a few errors in respect of the history of the house, the brochure printed specifically for the auction is a comprehensive guide to the house, and contains many items of interest. [84]

The house was described as "formerly the favourite Hunting Box of the thirteenth Earl of Derby", with an estate which "extends over an area of 180 acres, and comprises an exceedingly Picturesque Family Mansion in the castellated style, occupying a healthy yet sheltered situation about 375 feet above sea level, and commanding grand views of the diversified downlands and pastoral scenery of the district. The House contains Five Reception Rooms, Twenty Bed and Dressing Rooms, Two Bath Rooms, Commodious Domestic Offices and Cellarage. It is surrounded by the most Delightful Pleasure Grounds, interspersed with Ornamental Plantations, and including a Fine Stretch of Parkland. There are Two Lodge Entrances and a Well-appointed Set of Stabling for eight

The Oaks in 1912: the rear of the house showing alterations carried out by Joseph Smith and his unknown architect.

horses, with Coach House and Motor Garage; a handsome range of Conservatories and Greenhouses; Two additional Cottages for servants; also a Substantial and Commodious Modern Farmstead, Two Cottages and a Smithy." A short history of the house taken from Brayley introduced the interested buyer to some of the notable previous occupants, but included the thirteenth Earl of Derby instead of the twelfth.[84]

Other details in the brochure supplied the information that the property "is believed to be free from the payment of Land Tax, but is subject to Tithe Rent charge, the amount payable for the past year being £27: 17s: 2d., and to Undeveloped Land Duty amounting to £21: 3s: 3d. per annum. The Landlord also pays a sum of £30 per annum to the Sutton Water Company in respect of the water supplied to the Mansion, Farm and other properties on the Estate." [84]

The "Pleasure Grounds" then contained some fine cedars, American oaks and "other exotics", and were "remarkable" at the time of the sale for many ancient beeches. It was alleged that there was a spring in one of the beech trees near the house, because it always had water in it, although the well by which the mansion was supplied was three hundred feet deep. "However, the branches of this tree were so intertwisted that hollows were formed in the trunk, receiving and retaining rain water, which, from time to time, may be said to distil from the branches." The water from the well adjoining the house was raised by machinery worked by a horse, and conveyed to the top of the building. "The supply was copious and of the finest quality." [84]

Among the "residential amenities" were the local golf courses. The noted Walton Heath Golf Course was only about five miles distant, and "another excellent golf course is now on the point of completion at Woodcote Park, only one mile from the Property." The Banstead and Chipstead links were each about two miles away from The Oaks, and those at Purley and Mitcham, approximately three and four miles respectively. There were shooting and hunting amenities as well. "For its size, the property affords capital Shooting, while that in the neighbourhood includes good coverts." The Surrey Foxhounds and Surrey Staghounds hunted in the district, while the "Shooting" over the estate was let temporarily, but possession of it could be obtained on completion of the sale. [84]

Despite the good details of The Oaks and its estate in the brochure, it would seem likely that no satisfactory bids were made at the auction. Mrs. James continued to reside at the house for almost another two years, until her death occurred at the age of seventy-four in April, 1914, and she was buried at Woodmansterne. [65, 76]

Chapter 9
UNDER PUBLIC OWNERSHIP

After the death of Mrs. James, The Oaks and its estate were administered by a Mr. Lazares Marcus Lowenstein of Holborn Viaduct in London, who seems a likely executor of Mrs. James's will. On 3rd May, 1915, the Surrey Joint Poor Law Committee purchased all of the property from Mr. Lowenstein for the sum of £16,000. [85] The house then was used as a "Home for Women Epileptics", [86] and some minor interior alterations were made for that purpose, such as the addition of extra baths in the bathrooms. [87]

The Oaks was subsequently taken over by the Surrey County Council under the functions of the Local Government Act of 1929, [86] and a Requisition on the Title of the property was made by them on 6th July, 1933. It was recorded that "approximately fifty female sane epileptics" were then transferred to The Lodge at Effingham. [88] Soon afterwards, the mansion and its estate were purchased by the Carshalton Urban District Council on 18th July, 1933, for the sum of £41,800. [66, 76] The Council's decision to buy The Oaks had been made with the intention of "preserving for all time as much as possible of an Estate consisting of the most beautiful, natural parkland and woodland with historic associations dating back to the fourteenth century". Approximately eighty acres would be open to the public, and the remainder of the land let on a lease to a tenant farmer. [66]

In the first instance, the Council also had plans to sell off about one quarter of the estate for private building development, in order to recoup some of the money paid out for The Oaks. Such a decision, if implemented, would have meant the loss of a section of the present-day woodland walk adjoining Oakhurst Rise, as well as the land behind the belt of trees along Woodmansterne Road, up to the entrance to the park (now used by the Oaks Park Sports Centre for part of the nine and eighteen-hole golf courses, squash courts, the clubhouse and the car park). Expert advice was sought on how to make the best use of the lands in the Oaks Park to provide some sports facilities for the public. A report was made for this purpose in October, 1935, by Messrs. Dawson & partners, who described The Oaks thus: "One of the great charms of the park is its secluded and restful atmosphere, due to the encircling belt of really fine trees." Their comments on the proposal for the housing development were that these trees "would, doubtless, be incorporated and pierced only for access and exit", but they felt that the houses would destroy " all feelings of seclusion and the effect of natural beauty, and open country, in a rapidly developing area". It would restrict the space available for a proposed golf course, and interfere with the "encircling walk within the grounds". [89]

Messrs. Dawson & Partners suggested that the site of the old, walled-in kitchen ground opposite the Oaks Farm could be used for a swimming pool, with parking facilities in the farmyard on the other side of the lane. Elsewhere in the Oaks Park, the land available would provide for two association football grounds, a children's football ground, ten tennis courts (six hard and four grass) , two bowling greens, and one cricket table, as well as a golf course. The cost of these facilities, without the swimming pool, came to £20,010. [89]

Part of The Oaks mansion, and its immediate surroundings, could be used in connection with the proposed golf course. The position of the eighteenth green should be on the north lawn, and the large reception rooms in the east wing of the house used as a public restaurant and lounge, with ready access to the lawns on the south and east front, while the central portion facing north could be allotted to the Golf Club. It would also be advisable to reserve the north terrace and lawns for the golfers, and to enclose the area with a railing to prevent the public from straying on to the ground "devoted to golf". A path from the terrace on the north and west would lead through the woods to the first tee. Suggestions were made for conversions of the old store sheds, potting sheds, and other buildings at the rear of the demolished greenhouses into "excellent offices and workshops" for the golf professional and caddies, and the old farm buildings near the eighth tee into a store for tools, mowing machines, etc. The latter could be used as a "mixing place" for manures and other composts required for the upkeep of the greens and fairways. [89]

The total yardage of the proposed golf course as planned was 5,465 yards, and the estimated cost for it was £6,000. Previously, a suggestion had been made that the first and tenth tees should be sited near the Clubhouse, but the proposed new scheme would make available three starting places, the first, eighth and thirteenth holes, so that, on crowded days, these would be "a boon". [89, 90] (For the information of many of the present-day golfers who use the modern courses at the Oaks Park Sports Centre, the proposed yardages planned for the pre-war golf-course are set out in Appendix II.)

The plan to sell off one quarter of the Oaks Park for building purposes was abandoned. The Surrey County Council, and the old London County Council, each made grants of £7,000 to Carshalton Urban District Council towards the purchase price of the estate. Eventually, it was agreed to preserve the whole of the lands as part of London's Green Belt. [66] During the time in which the local Council was considering the proposals for the use of the parklands, some of the rooms on the ground, first and second floors of the house were opened to the public. Visitors were conducted round on guided tours, and were able to see the fire-places copied from Robert Adam's designs, the fine oak staircase, and the bedrooms, some of which had cupboards in the turrets. The special features were the beautiful dining-room attributed to Sir Robert Taylor, with its large fireplace, fluted Corinthian columns, coupled columns, and medallions on the walls, all of which were painted in white, blue and gold, and the Adam drawing-room. Both of these rooms were in the east wing. [87]

In pre-Second World War days, only the parkland immediately surrounding The Oaks mansion, together with the outer woodland walk, were available for use by the public.

The remainder of the park and downlands were used for farming purposes. The flower gardens near the house were kept well-stocked, and presented colourful displays of blooms throughout the spring, summer and autumn seasons. A variety of fish swam in the lily-pond by the "grotto" in the floral beds on the site of the old greenhouses. [87]

After the commencement of the Spanish Civil War in 1936, Carshalton Urban District Council provided rent-free accommodation at The Oaks mansion for a group of twenty-five children, most of whom had Basque Nationalist parents. They lived in the house for about another three years, until after the victory of General Franco, when peace was restored in their country, and some were allowed to return there before the Second World War began, [91] while others had to remain in Britain.

During the war, the Oaks Park and farmlands were used in the nation-wide campaign to "grow more food". By 1940, most of the windows of The Oaks had been covered over, and those on the ground-floor of the east wing were protected by large brick structures, in order to prevent damage from the blasts of any bombs which fell in its vicinity, especially during the Battle of Britain and the Blitz which started later that year. The house provided accommodation for the Local Defence Volunteers, who became D Company of the 55th Surrey Battalion Home Guard. [92]

The Oaks attracted the attention of the notorious "Lord Haw-Haw" - a nickname given to William Joyce, who broadcast to Britain from Germany every evening as part of the German campaign to destroy the confidence of the British people, especially during the threatened invasion period in 1940. Mr. Joyce had gained his fictitious title because of the most ludicrous lies he told, which became a constant source of amusement to the people who listened to him, after the BBC's programmes had closed down at night during the air-raids on south-eastern England, and elsewhere in Britain. According to him - and the more infamous Dr. Goebbels - the "Castle of the Oaks" was "the strongly-fortified hereditary keep of the Derby family, whence the constantly-repeated revolts of the ill-treated and exploited peasantry were bloodily suppressed." [93] Perhaps the doctor, and "Lord Haw-Haw", had read about the twelfth Earl of Derby's cook, who complained about preparing suppers at 3 am?

Despite the ridiculous statement made by Mr. Joyce about The Oaks, there can be little doubt that the Germans had made plans to destroy it if possible. As well as the occupation of the house by the local Home Guard, it also was used for periods by the Royal Air Force, and, later, as a military store by the Army, in their preparations for D-Day in 1944. Consequently, throughout the years from 1940 onwards, eleven high-explosive bombs, five V-1 flying-bombs, and numerous incendiaries, fell within the estate, and some of these exploded close enough to the mansion to cause a degree of damage to it. Also, considerable interior dilapidation increased at that time. [94] A Spitfire Mark II fighter plane, which was being given a brief air-test, crashed in the belt of trees surrounding the parklands,and not far from the mansion. Luckily, Pilot Officer Macphair, who was testing the aircraft, managed to bail out in time, but the cause of the crash has remained a mystery. [95]

After the cessation of all hostilities, and the end of the "grow more food" campaign, further fields on the north-western side of The Oaks were opened to the public to form the present-day Oaks Park, but those covered by today's golf courses continued to be used for farming purposes. However, the pre-war plans for the lay-out of the Park's sporting facilities never took place, and no repairs were carried out on the house to make it weather-proof. [96]

Chapter 10
THE END OF THE OAKS

During the immediate post-war years, Carshalton Urban District Council did not carry out any repairs to The Oaks mansion, and its condition slowly deteriorated, much to the consternation of a section of the public who were interested in the preservation of the house because of its important historical and architectural associations. Considerable interior dilapidation had taken place during, and after, the war, partly due to the bomb damage, to wear and tear from its wartime use, and to neglect by the Council. Loose slates on the roof allowed rain to seep through ceilings, most of the windows remained boarded over, and dry rot gradually increased. Thus, what had once been a unique, fine old house was slowly crumbling into a ruin. [96]

By 1953, the Council had given careful consideration to the future of the house, and consulted the Royal Fine Art Commission, the National Trust, the Ministry of Works, the Ministry of Town and Country Planning (Historical Buildings Section), the Surrey County Council, the Society for the Protection of Ancient Buildings, and the National Ancient Monuments Society.[94] In July, 1953, the Council's Petition for the grant of a Charter of Incorporation as a Municipal Borough described The Oaks in these terms:

"The mansion building is of middle and late eighteenth century work, with variations carried out in the nineteenth century. Earlier work cannot now be traced. The red brick exterior has been handled with mock castle tower and machiolated parapets somewhat in the manner of the period of Henry VII, and is considered to be interesting as a piece of original eighteenth century "Folly" architecture, of which only a limited number of examples of the period exist. [Machiolations were openings between the corbels of a projecting parapet for discharging missiles upon attackers.]

Internally, features of interest are two saloons on the ground floor, one being handled in the Adam style, and the other after the manner of John Nash or Sir John Soane. The ornamental plaster ceiling over the main oak staircase may be original late eighteenth century work.

A scheme is now being prepared for the preservation of the building, and for its adaptation, part as residential accommodation, part as a museum, and the remainder, including the saloons above mentioned, as a suite of rooms for receptions, civic or social functions." [94]

Continual discussions took place about the future of The Oaks mansion both at General Purposes Committee level, and at full Council meetings. An Oaks Sub-Committee was formed to deal with the problems, and this Committee's report, submitted to the Council

The Oaks after the Second World War showing the damage done during the war by nearby bombs, the wartime occupants and local vandals, and neglect by Carshalton Urban District Council. © Sport and General Press Agency.

on 23rd March, 1955, contained the information that the two stages of the proposed work to be carried out were:

1. Conversion of the west wing into four flats, and the weather-proofing of the whole building.

2. The repair and adaptation of the east wing to provide public rooms and facilities for catering, etc.

Although the Council had already approved these proposals, and the estimated cost for the first stage had been £8,500, by March, 1955, the sub-committee had been advised that the lowest tender for the work had risen to £18,500. Furthermore, the final account, probably, would be considerably above that price due to extra work required because of the dilapidated condition of the building. The Senior Regional Architect of the Ministry of Housing and Local Government had been consulted, and was fully conversant both with the house and the Council's proposals, but he had taken the view that his Department would be unlikely to give approval either for loan consent, or for an improvement grant for expenditure based on the lowest tender received.[97]

The estimate for Stage 2 was approximately £12,000, but the Council felt that if the cost showed an increase proportionate to that of Stage 1, there would be a commitment to very heavy expenditure. Also, the flats, although adequate, would not provide a standard of accommodation comparable with one normally envisaged by the Council. Even after the repairs and conversion work had been completed on the building as a whole, probably due to its age and construction, future maintenance costs would be high. The Oaks Sub-Committee had visited the mansion, and, after a thorough inspection, they were convinced that the deterioration which had taken place since the end of the war had reached such a stage that there was no justification for proceeding with the proposals for the repair and adaptation of the whole, or any part of the house. Although the mansion was included in a list of buildings of special architectural or historic interest, compiled by the Minister of Housing and Local Government under Section 3 of the Town and Country Planning Act, 1947, the sub-committee reluctantly concluded that the only course open was to endeavour to secure the removal of The Oaks from this list, so that it could be demolished as soon as possible. It was felt that it would not be unduly difficult to persuade the Ministry, and the Surrey County Council, to agree to this decision, in view of the mansion's deplorable condition. As yet, no detailed consideration had been given as to what could be done with the site. The Council might wish, at some later date, to provide a restaurant pavilion here, and to incorporate one or two of the better preserved fittings, such as fire surrounds, from the mansion, either in the new building, on in other existing buildings in the Council's ownership, as a suitable reminder of the former historic associations of The Oaks.[97]

The Council's decision to seek authority to demolish The Oaks was not received with enthusiasm by the Surrey County Council, who reported it to the County Records and

The drawing-room designed by Robert Adam, showing detail of the frieze and cornice, before the demolition of The Oaks. RCHME Crown Copyright.

Ancient Monuments Committee, and hoped that some use could be found for the mansion. Also, the County Council suggested that an approach be made to the recently-instituted Historic Buildings Bureau operating under the Historic Buildings Council for England, at the Ministry of Works, and set up to compile a list of, and , possibly, find an appropriate use for, eligible buildings threatened with demolition.[98]

Carshalton Urban District Council wrote to the Historic Buildings Bureau, who replied pointing out that the only premises for which they endeavoured to find uses were those upon which they had received express instruction form the Historic Buildings Council, and had forwarded the letter to them for consideration. They, in turn, replied, pointing out that, under the Historic Buildings and Ancient Monuments Act, 1953, the Minister of Works was empowered to make grants towards the cost of the repair and maintenance of buildings of architectural or historical interest, and the local Council's letter would be taken as an application for a grant, which would be considered at a meeting on the 12th May, 1955.[98]

The Ministry of Housing and Local Government wrote to Carshalton Urban District Council stating that The Oaks was a building of very considerable architectural interest and importance. The Ministry would like to see it preserved, if possible, and suggested that the Society for the Protection of Ancient Buildings, who had considerable experience in the restoration and conversion of historic buildings in an economical and practical way, might be able to estimate for the work on the house at a cheaper price than the tenders already obtained by the Council. Therefore, the Society should be consulted before a decision was made to demolish the building. If required, the Ministry offered the services of their technical officers.[98]

Finally, the Society for the Protection of Ancient Buildings wrote to the local Council suggesting consultations, with a view to evolving a satisfactory scheme for the renovation of the mansion. The Council's General Purposes Committee authorised the further consultations to find out whether there was any prospect of a substantial grant being made towards the necessary repairs on The Oaks.[98]

During the period from June, 1955, until July, 1956, while discussions and consultations on the fate of The Oaks took place, the condition of the house slowly deteriorated even further. The Minister of Works had agreed, on certain conditions, to grant the sum of £5,000 towards the restoration of the mansion, and £1,000 had been received in compensation of damage caused to the building during wartime occupation, as well as a payment in the region of £6,000 made by the War Damage Commission. However, prices for the Council"s proposed schemes for the future use of the house, including the repair work, had risen to an estimated cost of £54,000.[99]

On 23rd May, 1956, a chimney stack measuring eight feet long, seven or eight feet high, and eighteen inches wide, in the centre of the east wing of the mansion, collapsed and crashed through the roof of the flat formerly occupied by the caretaker, carrying away the

The drawing-room, showing one of the fireplaces attributed to Robert Adam, photographed prior to the demolition of The Oaks. RCHME Crown Copyright.

floor and ceiling beneath it, and falling into the "Regency"room (drawing-room) on the south side of the east wing. Other parts of the ornamental brickwork on the roof parapet were brought down at the same time, and the structure of this section of the building was severely shaken. The Council's Engineer and Surveyor was urgently requested to arrange for the east wing to be roped off, and danger notices to be exhibited. Also, part of the remaining unstable brickwork had to be demolished, and the rest of it made safe.[99]

The Engineer and Surveyor reported that other parts of the mansion were in imminent danger of collapse. Mr.David Nye, the architect who had inspected the building in 1950, and again in 1955, on behalf of the Society for the Protection of Ancient Buildings, had submitted his report dated 13th October, 1955, in which he pointed out that the fabric of the house had deteriorated since his previous visit. There were numerous outbreaks of fungal decay, ceilings had collapsed in various rooms, and beams and main supporting joists had decayed, and were unsafe. Mr. Nye thought that most of The Oaks should be demolished, leaving the ground floor public rooms in the east wing, and forming a new roof, with parapet walls, at the lower level. These rooms could be used as a small restaurant and cloakrooms, and their preservation would retain a link with the former mansion. However, in view of the further deterioration, the Engineer and Surveyor was asked to submit a report on the practicability of demolishing the whole of the house (except the outbuildings) west of the entrance hall; also demolishing the remainder down to first floor level and roofing in the remaining structure by covering the floors of what had been the first floor rooms with roofing felt, thus removing any danger to the public, and take into consideration Mr. Nye's suggestions. Any items of architectural merit, such as fireplaces, hall panelling, etc. should be stripped out, and could be used in future in the new restaurant suite, or in some other Council property. Arrangements for the work had to be treated as a matter of urgency, and advice on it obtained by consultations with Messrs. Ebenezer Mears & Son, who were specialist demolition contractors.[99]

An application was made to the Ministry of Housing and Local Government, and the Surrey County Council, for permission to proceed with the proposed demolition works, and tenders were obtained from a selected panel of demolition contractors.[100] Enquiries were made to the Ministry of Works as to whether their grant of £5,000 previously offered would still be available for the revised scheme. However, after the Minister had received the advice of the Historic Buildings Council, he decided that he would not be justified in offering any grant towards the cost of this scheme! At the same time, the Beddington, Carshalton and Wallington Archaeological Society had suggested that a photographic record should be made of the interior of the mansion, both before, and during, the demolition work. The Council's Senior Engineering Assistant, Mr. L. Wilson, had already taken a set of twenty-one photographs of the interior of The Oaks.[101]

By the end of October, 1956, the Council had been informed by the Ministry of Housing and Local Government that the Chief Investigator of Historic Buildings had reported to the Advisory Committee on Buildings of Special Architectural and Historic Interest, and had recommended that the Council's proposals for The Oaks should be accepted in view

The entrance hall of The Oaks, looking east, just before demolition.
RCHME Crown Copyright.

of the state of the building. He also recommended the retention of the turreted south front of the east wing to its full height, and the Advisory Committee had suggested that, if possible, the ceiling in the staircase hall should be retained. The Minister had accepted this advice, and raised no objections to the Council's scheme. The Surrey County Council then issued formal planning permission for the work on the understanding that careful consideration would be given to the suggestions made.[102]

Subsequently, The Oaks Sub-Committee were advised that the suggested retention of the east wing did not present any difficulties, and it had been included in the work put out for tender. Regretfully, the conclusion was reached that it was impracticable to retain the ceiling in the staircase hall, and the Ministry should be informed accordingly. The lowest tender for the partial demolition of the house at a cost of £1,669 was submitted by the Demolition and Construction Company Limited, and accepted.[103]

Demolition work began on The Oaks in December, 1956, and, as it proceeded, it became evident that the structural condition of the whole building was even worse than originally anticipated.[104] The foreman of the contractors reported that the mansion "was the worst building he had demolished in his twenty-three years of experience". The bricks used in its construction "were so soft" that they could not be used elsewhere. He also stated that one of the corner turrets added by the twelfth Earl of Derby had not been keyed into the adjacent wall, and was in a very unstable condition.[105] As a result, the Council concluded that the required renovations and improvements to the east wing for the proposed restaurant would prove costly, and out of all proportion to the value of these rooms as "a nucleus for public use". Therefore, it was felt that the whole of the remainder of the mansion should be demolished, with the exception of the "Adam" room (dining-room) on the ground floor, as its architectural merit deserved preservation and it was less affected by the dilapidations than the remaining rooms. Arrangements were made for an urgent inspection of the residue of the building by Inspectors from the Ministry of Housing and Local Government and the Surrey County Council.[104]

The Council's Engineer and Surveyor then submitted a scheme whereby parts of The Oaks could be preserved according to a suggestion made by the Ministry of Housing and Local Government and the Surrey County Council. It would involve putting a roof on the "Adam" room, as well as building a new kitchen and cloakrooms adjacent to it, while the turreted portion here would be preserved as previously requested. The estimated cost of the work was £8,500, but, if the work was held over until a later date, it was essential for authority to be given for an immediate expenditure of approximately £500 to cover the cost of treating the false framework to the "Adam" room with some suitable preservative.[106]

The Oaks Sub-Committee of the Council considered the Engineer and Surveyor's proposals, but felt that his scheme was too costly. He was requested to prepare new estimates for carrying out the minimum amount of work necessary to preserve the "Adam" room and the turreted portion of the building, as required by the Ministry and the

Demolition of The Oaks in progress.

County Council, to whom the revised plans should be submitted when available. Also, it had to be pointed out to them that, in view of the costs involved, the rate-payers of Carshalton should not be expected to bear the expense. Therefore, if these sections of the building were to be preserved, then the necessary monies had to be made available to the local Council.[106]

At the end of November, 1958, most of The Oaks had been demolished, and only the east wing was left standing on the site. The Ministry and County Council had not responded to the Council's request for financial assistance to preserve and restore the "Adam" room. Consequently, a decision was made to apply to them for consent for the demolition of the remainder of the building, and for the Engineer and Surveyor to invite tenders for the work. He pointed out that, if the necessary authority to demolish was obtained, then there were certain features such as fireplaces and wall decorations which might be of considerable value if they were removed and incorporated in another building. The Oaks Sub-Committee all agreed that they knew of no such building under the Council's control, but they felt that endeavours should be made to dispose of these articles at the best price obtainable, preferably within the county of Surrey, or elsewhere in the Home Counties. The officers of the Council were then instructed to make a provisional approach to the County Council on this matter.[107]

The Minister of Housing and Local Government raised no further objections to the Council's decision to demolish the remaining portion of The Oaks, [108] and neither did the County Records Historic Buildings and Antiquities Committee, who felt unable to recommend that the Surrey County Council purchase the period features in the building.[109] These were offered for sale to the highest bidder, and the closing date of 20th February, 1959, for any bids, was selected to appear in the public advertisement, the responses to which were considered by The Oaks Sub-Committee.[110,111] Finally, it was decided to accept the offer of £375 made by Messrs. John Rushton and Company of Wallington, who became the new owners of these articles from the mansion.[112]

The Surrey County Council, who were the Local Planning Authority at that time, decided not to raise any objections to the Council's proposal to demolish the remains of the house. Instead, they asked to be informed when the work was completed, so that the Ministry of Housing and Local Government could be requested to delete the building from the statutory list .[113]

By the end of November, 1959, a tender in the sum of £561: 10s: 0d., submitted by Messrs. Charles Griffiths Limited, had been accepted for the demolition work.[114] Although they had started to demolish the remaining portion of The Oaks on 16th November, they found that one turret could not be dismantled until an electrical installation in it had been removed.[115] Eventually, the site was cleared, and only the outbuildings belonging to the mansion were left as a reminder of an important, and irreplaceable, part of our local heritage, which had been removed from the Oaks Park.

Unveiling the Home Guard seat, Oaks Park, 23rd October 1955.

Chapter 11
THE OAKS PARK AND SPORTS CENTRE

$\mathbf{I}$n the post -war years, the Oaks Park became a popular place for members of the public to visit, and enjoy the peaceful, rural atmosphere of the parklands, as well as the woodland walk in the outer belt of trees. The floral displays at the southern end of the park, and in the flower-beds by the "Grotto" on the site of the green-houses, were an added attraction throughout the spring, summer and autumn seasons. Light refreshments could be bought at a small tea-hut on the western side of the outbuildings of The Oaks mansion.[96]

In the early 1950s, the Council made a short horse-ride in part of the outer belt of trees from the East Lodge entrance to the park up to an iron field-gate near the cross-roads at the Oaks Corner. Horses and riders then went out on to Woodmansterne Road, and proceeded along Croydon Lane to the bridleway up to Banstead Downs (the traffic on these roads was much lighter in those days).[96] The first ride was led by Mr. H. Cowleshaw and a group of his pupils from his riding-school at Carshalton on the Hill (by the allotments at the rear of Stanley Road and Cranfield Road West).[116] At the end of that decade, the horse-ride was extended from the East Lodge to the bridle-way at the northern end of the parklands by Oakhurst Rise. In recent years, and for the safety of both horses and riders, it has been made possible for them to ride around the circumference of the park, and part of the golf-course, without using any of the public highways.

During the period in which the fate of The Oaks mansion was being debated by the Council, a seat commemorating the wartime occupation of the house by 'D' Company of the 55th Surrey Battalion of the Home Guard was erected on the front lawn. The seat's unveiling ceremony took place in 1955, and was performed by the Clerk of the Council in the summer of that year. Among the crowd in attendance were many of the men who had served in 'D' Company, and who had memories of their duties here.[117] Unfortunately, the plaque on the seat has been removed by vandals since then, and recently the seat itself has been re-sited on the western side of the lawns. Members of the Home Guard had formed a Masonic Lodge in 1944, and had called themselves "The Oaks Lodge". They adopted a rugged, ancient oak tree as their badge.[118]

In 1957, the Oaks Park became the venue for an international caravan rally, and included members from the Caravan Club of Great Britain. [117] The event was well-attended, and enjoyed by everyone, including the on-lookers, who were mostly local residents. Also, the Guides and Scouts were allowed to hold their camps in the park each year, and, later, were given a camp-site to use in the woods where the old game-keeper's cottage once stood.[96]
..

Part of the International Caravan Rally in the Oaks Park 1959.

At the end of December, 1959, after being informed that the completion of all of the demolition work on The Oaks was imminent, the Council's General Purposes Committee decided to ask the Public Pleasure Grounds and Allotments Committee to consider the possibility of providing more suitable facilities, on a moderate scale, for the provision of refreshments to the public using the Oaks Park. More adequate housing accommodation for members of the park's staff permanently employed there was also requested.[115] The East and South Lodges at the entrances to the park were each occupied then by a park-keeper and his family. Consequently, a new café and toilet facilities replaced the small tea-hut and old toilets, and the lodges were demolished and replaced by two houses on each of their sites during the following years, and before Carshalton Urban District Council, together with the Boroughs of Beddington and Wallington, and Sutton and Cheam, became amalgamated to form the London Borough of Sutton in 1965.[96]

The fields on the western side of the Oaks Park continued to be used for farming purposes by tenant farmers for a few more years, during which time the South Eastern Gas Board laid a section of the outer London ring main along the southern side of the woodland walk of the park's outer belt of trees, and across the farmlands of the Oaks Farm.[96] A Deed of Grant of Easement between the London Borough of Sutton and the Gas Board was made out on 23rd March, 1971, while an agreement for aerial markers was completed in the same year.[76]

Plans to revive the sporting tradition connected with The Oaks were put into action in 1972, when the farmlands on the west side of the park were taken over for an eighteen-hole golf course, with a small, nine-hole pitch and putt one, for use by the public. The land was leased from Sutton Council by Messrs. Alphagreen Limited, and the 6,183-yard course was designed by a golf course architect, Mr. John Day.[119]

After the golf-course had been constructed by Alphagreen who have managed it since then, and although it was estimated that the whole course would take about two years to settle down, it was opened early in response to public demand.[119] The first person to tee off here on Monday, 2nd July, 1973, was Mr. Percy Stock of Pine Ridge, Carshalton. Mr. Stock was seventy-eight years old, and had campaigned for years to have a golf course in the Oaks Park. He was followed on the first tee by the youngest member of the players, Miss Hilary Moon of Mead Crescent in Sutton. Later, the official opening ceremony was performed at the end of September, 1973. The Council had fixed the club rates at 88 pence per round on week-days, and £1.43 at weekends and public holidays. Both prices were inclusive of VAT.[120]

On 25th March, 1974, a lease of the golf course for a period of forty-two years was made out between the London Borough of Sutton and Alphagreen Limited, and it came into force on 19th January, 1976. By then, the new Sports Centre had become very popular with the local golfers, and its popularity increased when a Squash Club was opened here on 30th November, 1976.[119] It soon became evident that these facilities needed expanding, and more squash courts were added to the existing ones, while a nine-hole course had replaced the smaller pitch and putt one by the beginning of the 1980s. Subsequently, both the clubhouse and the golf shop here also have been enlarged, and a golf driving-range was opened in the autumn of 1982.

Meanwhile, the bi-centenary of the Fête Champêtre held at The Oaks occurred on 9th June, 1974. To mark the occasion, the Carshalton Society persuaded the London Borough of Sutton's Arts Council to stage a revival of John Burgoyne's play, *The Maid of The Oaks*. Thus, three performances of the London stage version took place in the open air here on 7th and 8th June, 1974, and were directed by June Voller. However, the audience's enjoyment of the end of the last performance on 8th June was spoilt by a thunderstorm.[121]

By 1981, the Department of the Environment had decided to include the outbuildings of The Oaks mansion, and "The Grotto" on the site of the span of greenhouses, in the list of Buildings of Special Architectural or Historic Interest. In November, 1981,these became Grade II listed buildings - a decision which was praised by the historians. For some years, the outbuildings consisting of the old stables, double coach-house, a large garage, and the grooms' and chauffeur's quarters, have been used by local theatrical companies as their workshops, and for storage of their scenery.[122,123]

Early in 1985, the Council decided to cut down the remains of one of the large old Lambert's Oaks, which stood on the western edge of the top lawn of the park, and had been damaged when vandals had started a fire in its hollow interior. The Chairman of the Carshalton Society, Mr. Gordon Rookledge, visited the Oaks Park one Sunday and found that most of the tree, except for the base of the main trunk, had been removed to the Council's bonfire site adjacent to the park's front lawns. Early on the following morning, Mrs. Rookledge contacted the workman tending the bonfire, and was allowed to take away four of the oak logs. Afterwards, these were exhibited at the 1985 Sutton Green Fair.[124]

Because of the historical importance of the old oak tree, and its associations with the twelfth Earl of Derby's sporting seat, and the Oaks and Derby races on Epsom Downs, Mr. Rookledge took the logs to Oakcraft's oak timber sawmills at Bolney in Sussex. The Carshalton Society requested an estimate from Oakcraft for the quantity and costs of producing and packaging carved plaques of, for example, The Oaks mansion, Epsom Grandstand, a horse and jockey, some stables, a winning post and a horse-shoe. The Society was informed that the great age of the wood precluded production of carved statuettes from it, a matter about which they had also enquired.[124]

The Carshalton Society decided to try and find an outlet, or outlets, for the sale of the plaques before any work commenced on them,, Consequently, in June and July, 1985, letter were sent to the Jockey Club and the National Horseracing Museum. The former was not interested, but although the Museum was not in a position to embark on the sale of the plaques, it was suggested that contact should be made with Ever Ready Batteries, who were the sponsors of the Oaks race, or with the owners of Epsom racecourse, United

Racecourses Limited, or Gilby Racing.[124]

Ever Ready's response was that they were unable to budget for the suggested plaques, and then a letter was sent to United Racecourses Limited on 11th November, 1985, informing them about the oak logs and the possible uses for the wood from them: also, the fact that these could be marketed with a certificate of authenticity signed by a representative of the Carshalton Society and, perhaps, the Jockey Club. In his reply, the Managing Director, Mr. Tim Neligan, pointed out that whilst United Racecourses would probably not be in a position to market the plaques, he would be happy to discuss the matter in general terms, and, possibly, refer it to Lord Derby.[124]

In a telephone conversation between Mr. Neligan and Mr. Rookledge, an alternative suggestion was put forward by Mr. Neligan that blocks made from the wood might be incorporated in the flooring of the proposed new grandstand. Mr. Rookledge wrote to Mr. Neligan on 9th December, 1985, to inform him that enough timber had been saved from the oak tree to make between two hundred and five hundred small blocks if required. The logs were stored at an oak timber sawmill in Sussex, and the Carshalton Society would be willing to sell these to United Racecourses Limited with letters confirming their authenticity, and photographs of the tree from which they were taken.[124]

In his letter of 15th January, 1986, Mr. Neligan told Mr. Rookledge that United Racecourses' sponsors (Ever Ready Batteries) had decided to issue a plaque, but made of porcelain, not wood. However, bearing in mind the plan for a new complex at the Epsom Racecourse in the near future, the timber from the oak tree could be incorporated in some form into the new building, similarly to the then current presentation of the brass bell used to start the first Derby race in 1780. Therefore, United Racecourse Limited would be prepared to purchase the logs for a modest price.[124]

Subsequently, in correspondence with Mr. E.C. Hamilton of Oakcraft, Mr. Rookledge was informed that a wood-carver had been supplied with a thin slice of the oak logs. Mr. Hamilton had been pleased to find that, on cutting the wood, it was a brown oak, fairly rare, and rather attractive. The saved logs were unique, and because of their novelty and historic interest, they should be insured for about one thousand pounds.[124]

Between August and December, 1986, negotiations took place between Mr. Rookledge and Mr. Neligan for the sale of the oak logs. Finally, after Mr. Neligan's visit to Oakcraft's timber sawmill, the Carshalton Society received a cheque for five hundred pounds, and were informed that Mr. Hamilton was making some sections of parquet flooring from the wood. These would be kept in store for United Racecourses Limited until they could be incorporated in the new grandstand at Epsom. Mr. Rookledge requested three pieces of the flooring - one each for himself, the Carshalton Society and the London Borough of Sutton - because of their historical importance.[124] (At the time of

The east drive in Oaks Park near the restaurant, before the hurricane in October 1987.

going to press, it is still hoped that the blocks made from the logs will be put in the floor of the exhibition room of the new grandstand.)

The Sutton Conservation Group, which was formed in 1986, have included the Oaks Park in their activities since then. Organised nature walks are held in the outer woodland walk, as well as in the parklands, where items of interest in respect of the local flora and fauna are pointed out to members of the public participating in these guided tours. In the summer of 1987, the Group put up bird and bat boxes to encourage more wildlife into the park.[125]

Although it took several years for the late Carshalton Urban District Council to reach a decision about the demolition of The Oaks mansion, nature took only a few hours in which to devastate the parklands, when the infamous hurricane of 16th October, 1987 swept across south-eastern England, over the Surrey hills and down into the London Borough of Sutton, early on that day. Fifteen thousand trees were lost in the Oaks Park and some of them fell across Croydon Lane and Woodmansterne Road. Both roads were closed to traffic for many days, until the teams of tree-surgeons, brought in from the Midlands to help the Council's workmen, cleared away the debris and made safe the remnants of the woodlands bordering on to these highways. Hardly one in five trees remained standing in the woods at the southern end of the park, and the walk in the outer belt of trees was a scene of devastation, remaining unusable for about a year afterwards. The golf courses also were affected, but play resumed soon after the day of the storm.[126, 127]

The Council decided to include public support in the tree replacement programme and the first tree-planting ceremony took place in the park soon after the storm. Most of these young trees unfortunately did not survive, but subsequent plantings have had better chances of survival.

The tremendous task of removing the fallen trees began in 1988. The scene of devastation has been slow to improve, and still looks very open, especially in the winter months. The horse-ride and the public bridleways were cleared of debris so that these could be used again by local riding shcools and other horse-riders. Spring and summer seasons bring forth many new species of flowers in the remains of the woodlands, and include some garden varieties, which were blown here during the storm and add their colours to those of the wild ones to offer some compensation to the regular visitors to the park.

Since 1986, the Council has entered the annual "London in Bloom" competition, and produced some good displays in the flowerbeds near the small restaurant and those on the site of the old greenhouses known as "The Grotto." The latter survived the damage caused by the hurricane, although the large cedar tree on the opposite lawn was blown down, and some of its branches fell across the path and flowerbeds recently planted for the 1988 spring display.

In the early summer of 1989, the Croydon Aviation Research Group, who had spent the previous eight years searching for the remnants of planes which crashed in the Second World War, found the remains of the Spitfire Mark II that fell out of the sky during its test flight, and landed in the outer woodland belt of trees in the park, about fifty years ago. Members of the Group had searched these woods for months without success, until they were contacted by an original eye-witness of the crash, and were led to the precise location of it. The Council gave permission for them to dig in this area, and cleared it of undergrowth for them. Their finds included some perspex from the cockpit canopy, armoured glass from the windshield, two instrument faces from the speedometer and the oil/temperature gauge, three sections of the control columns, parts of the dashboard and the engine, as well as a section of the wooden propeller. At that time, they were trying to trace more details about the pilot, whose name was Macphair, and who was believed to have survived the war.[128]

In 1990, the hurricane-force gales of late January and early February claimed more victims from the large, older trees in the park and on the golf course. However, the damage done by the storms has not affected the numbers of visitors to the parklands, or the popularity of the Sports Centre. Members of the Carshalton and Wallington Art Society, who hold an annual display of their work on each August Bank Holiday Monday, have continued to exhibit their paintings for sale near the restaurant and south drive, although space was limited here before the fallen trees were cleared away after the hurricane in October, 1987. Tree-planting continues in the woodlands, but it will take many years for the saplings to mature.

One Friday afternoon in September, 1990, a group of one hundred and seventy-five people in seventy cars gathered in the Oaks Park before setting off on a sponsored week-end fund-raising event, the Chass aux Trésors (Treasure Hunt) held in Normandy, France, in aid of the National Society for the Prevention of Cruelty to Children (NSPCC) and St. Catherine's Hospice in Crawley, Sussex. The Mayor and Mayoress of the London Borough of Sutton, Councillor and Mrs. John Brennan, hosted the send-off, which was held after the participants had partaken of the free ale, wines and cheese, in the marquee used as a beer tent and a French bar. Also present were representatives from the two charities (the NSPCC and the Hospice) together with local press reporters and photographers.[129]

The rally/treasure hunt/motorised crossword had been thought up towards the end of 1989, and was organised by Malcolm Coomber and his team from Clarkson Hyde, an accountancy, consultancy, and investigations firm in Sutton. Among the cars taking part in the 1990 event were three Porsche 911s, a Rolls-Royce, an Aston Martin Vantage Volante, a BMW 635 csi, a Mercedes Benz 500 SL, a Lotus Espirit Turbo SE, a Ferrari and a Triumph TR3.[129]

The cars set off for Portsmouth, where they were joined by others, including an old Citroen Light 1.5 (similar to the one used by the fictional French detective, Maigret). After an overnight journey to Cherbourg on the ferry, the contestants disembarked at 6 a.m. on Saturday morning, and the competition commenced making use of the maps itinerary, a list of fifteen objects to collect en route, and a three-page forty-five question document, which had been provided by the organisers. The route included Bayeux, where two hours were allowed for a visit to the famous Tapestry, and another stop-over was made at Le Mont St. Michel before setting off to arrive at St. Malo by 8. p.m. to hand in the competition forms. Then a special dinner was held for all of the competitors, who had been accommodated in five hotels within St. Malo's walled "old town". [129]

As a result of the sponsored Treasure Hunt, the Clarkson Hyde Charity Committee raised £12,000 for the two charities. Because of the success of the event, the Committee decided to hold another Chasse aux Trésors in 1991, for two hundred participants, who, after a mayoral send-off from the Oaks Park on Friday, 4th October, would travel via Portsmouth and Le Mont St. Michel to a *fruits de mer* reception in St. Malo. The most successful contestants could win a "romantic" five-day holiday in Paris. Also a "Charity Auction" of items generously donated for the event had been arranged for the evening of 5th October 1991, at the Hotel de France et Chateaubriand in St. Malo, and hosted by the Radio Mercury Disc Jockey, Russell Pocket. St. Catherine's Hospice in Crawley, Sussex, the St. Raphael's Hospice in North Cheam, Surrey, and the NSPCC, had been chosen as the Charities for 1991. [129]

Today, there are still some reminders of the important, historical past of the Oaks Park, and these can be seen at the southern end of the parklands. A section of the sunken fence (ha-ha) can be found on the northern edge of the top lawn, and, recently, more of it has been exposed after the clearance of the trees damaged in the gales of early 1990. The outbuildings and an old wash-house mark the site of The Oaks mansion. Near the restaurant, the "Grotto" wall at the rear of the flowerbeds shelters the plants from the cold northerly winds. The late eighteenth-century "Model Farmery" stands in a small valley on the south side of Croydon Lane, and, opposite to it are the remains of the large, walled garden. Nearby, a brick and flint cottage is situated on the edge of the golf course and the ruins of a well-house are on the adjoining fifteenth fairway.

It is sad that, through earlier neglect, there are only a few remnants of the building which was of so much historical importance both to the locality and to the nation.

The Oaks Mansion and its Estate in 1912.

The following details have been taken from the brochure prepared for the sale by auction of The Oaks on 12th July, 1912, at 2 p.m. , at The Mart, Tokenhouse Yard, London. The auctioneers were Messrs. Walton & Lee of 10, Mount Street, Grosvenor Square, and the estate agents were Messrs. Robert W. Fuller, Moon & Fuller, of 83, High Street, Croydon.

THE RESIDENCE

is approached by two winding Carriage Drives, each having an appropriate one-storey Lodge at the entrance; it is entered beneath an arched Portico and contains the following principal apartments on the Ground Floor level:-

Entrance and Staircase Hall

measuring about 30 ft. 8 in. by 16 ft. 3 in. and 29 ft. in height and having a oak dado and floor;

Side Hall with Corridor

leading to the

Dining Room

(South-East), a very fine apartment about 42 ft. 6 in. by 21 ft. 6 in. and 19 ft. in height, and handsomely decorated from designs by Robert Adam [sic].

Drawing Room

(South, South East and South West) about 39 ft. 2 in. inclusive of two fireplace recesses, by 33 ft. 3 in . and about 14 ft. 9 in. in height, and having lobbies in the turrets in the three angles of the room.

Billiard Room

(North-East) about 24 ft. 3 in., inclusive of a wide bay, by 23 ft. 6 in. and 14 ft. 9 in. high.

Smoking Room

(South West) about 16 ft. by 13 ft. 6 in., having two lobbies in the turrets, one of which is connected with the Post Office Telephone system; and a Lavatory with two basins, having hot and cold supplies and W.C. adjoining.

Each of the principal Reception Rooms and Hall has one or more Casement Windows opening to the Lawns , and a polished oak floor; and the Dining and Drawing Rooms and the Corridor leading to the latter apartment are heated by radiators.

Morning Room

(North East) about 18 ft. by 15 ft. and 14 ft. 9 in. in height.

The Fine Oak Staircase

has carvings and decorations in the 'Adam' style with a dado to match that in the Entrance Hall. Leading off the Half-Landing is a

Principal Bed Room

(North East) about 23 ft. 6 in. by 13 ft. 3 in., having two cupboard recesses in the turrets.

ON THE FIRST FLOOR:

In the main Eastern and Southern wings of the Mansion are:-

Upper Hall,

Two Principal Bed Rooms

(North West) measuring about 24 ft. 9 in. inclusive of bay, by 24 ft. , and 18 ft. by 14 ft. 6 in. respectively, the former fitted with a 'Well' fireplace and adapted for use as a Library.

Another Principal Bed Room

(North West) about 24 ft. 6 in. inclusive of bay, by 24 ft. 3 in.

Principal Bed Room

(East) with Dressing Room adjoining; the former measuring about 19 ft. 6 in. by 17 ft. 9 in.; W.C.; and a Suite comprising

Principal Bed Room

(South) about 20 ft. by 17 ft. 9 in., having Telephone laid on, and fitted with hanging cupboard.

Dressing Room,

Bath Room with porcelain-lined bath and lavatory basin, each with hot and cold supplies; W.C. and Maid's Bed Room.

Housemaids' Cupboard with lead-lined sink and cold supply.

In the Secondary, or Central and Western Wings, and also on the First Floor level, and reached by a separate staircase are:-

Housekeeper's Room,

A Secondary Bed Room,

Bath Room
with Bath in mahogany enclosure, having hot and cold services; Servant's Bed Room, and a Large Store Room and Linen Cupboard.

ON THE SECOND FLOOR:
and in the wings last referred to, are:-

Day and Night Nurseries
(South and North West) measuring respectively about 22 ft. 9 in. by 17 ft., and 24 ft. by 13 ft. 6 ins.,, the latter having Two Cupboards in the turrets and another range of Cupboards at the side, and a hanging Cupboard.

Housemaid's Bed Room or Work Room
with two cupboards in the turrets;

Four Servants' Bed Rooms,
and Housemaid's Room fitted with slop and washing-up sinks, having hot and cold supplies, and a range of cupboards.

ON THE THIRD FLOOR :-
In the central portion of the building are:-

A Large Bed Room for Servants,
Bed or Box Room and W.C.

The Domestic Offices
are placed entirely on the Ground Floor Level in the Central and Western sections of the building and comprise:- Butler's Pantry with glazed-ware sink, having hot and cold supplies; Strong Room with fittings by Chatwood; Lofty Kitchen about 20 ft. 3 in. square, having triple-oven 'Eagle' range; Scullery with small range and sink with hot and cold services; Servants' Hall about 21 ft. 10 in. by 17
....

ft; Larder having its walls lined with white glazed tiles; Dairy similarly fitted and having water laid on; China Closet, Boot Hole; Pump House; Game Larder; large Wash-house with copper, baking oven and sink with cold supply; Wood and Store places; and W.C.

Below the Residence are:-

Spacious Dry and Cool Cellars
for Champagne, Wine, Beer and general storage purposes.

SUMMER OF ACCOMMODATION:

Entrance Hall
Side Hall
Dining Room
Drawing Room
Morning Room
Billiard Room
Smoking Room
Lavatory and W.C.
Upper Hall
Six Principal Bed Rooms
Two Dressing Rooms
Two Bath Rooms And Four W.C's.
Day and Night Nurseries
Ten Secondary and Servants' Bed Rooms
Housekeeper's Room
Domestic Offices
Underground Cellarage

WATER. Water is laid on from the Sutton District Water Company's mains, and there is a large rain water tank beneath the Kitchen Yard.

HEATING. The Dining and Drawing Rooms and the Corridor leading to the latter apartment are heated by hot water from a furnace with boiler in the cellars. The water to the Baths and Lavatories is heated from the Kitchen range.

LIGHTING. The Mansion is lighted throughout by Acetylene Gas generated on the premises. This light is also installed to the Stables.

DRAINS. The Drains from the Mansion and Stables are taken to discharge into a cesspool fitted with chain pump in the Park. The effluent from the Farmery is disposed of so as to be available for use in the Kitchen Gardens.

The Telephone is laid into the Mansion, and there is a Post Box near South Lodge.

The nearest Church is at Woodmansterne about Three-Quarters-of-a-mile distant.

RESIDENTIAL AMENITIES

GOLF. The noted Walton Heath Golf Course is only about 5 miles distant, and another excellent Course is now on the point of completion at Woodcote Park, only 1 mile from the Property; Banstead and Chipstead Links are each about 2 miles distant, and those at Purley and Mitcham about 3 and 4 miles respectively.

SHOOTING AND HUNTING. For its size the property affords capital Shooting, while that in the neighbourhood includes good coverts. The Surrey Foxhounds and the Surrey Staghounds hunt the district.

The Roads

in the vicinity of the property are in excellent condition for motoring and the Banstead Downs afford exceptional facilities for riding exercise. Epsom Racecourse is about $4^1/_2$ miles South-West of the estate.

The Excellent Modern Stabling

is comprised in a brick and slated building, and includes Four Large Loose Boxes, and Four Stalls, with fittings by the St. Pancras Iron Works; Double Coach house with loft over; Saddle and Harness Rooms; and Two Grooms' Bed Rooms; and on the opposite side of the stable yard is a

Capital Garage

for three large cars, with pit, and heated by hot water; a petrol store and

Chauffeur's Cottage

containing four rooms. Adjacent to the foregoing are Bicycle House, Acetylene Gas House, Carbide Stores and two W.Cs.

The Stabling and Garage are lighted by acetylene gas and amply supplied with water.

The Gardens and Pleasure Grounds

are fully matured and have been laid out with great taste and judgement. The Plantations surrounding the House are intersected by the most delightful Wilderness Walks, leading towards the West to the handsome range of Conservatories, and Green Houses with a Rosery in front, while beyond is a Rose Border enclosed by clipped yew and laurel hedges. Across the Lawn towards the North, is a well-formed Tennis Court. In a secluded clump near the Residence is a spacious Aviary, and in the Wood at the rear is an old established Rookery.

The excellent Walled Kitchen and Fruit Garden

is situate on the South Western side of the House with entrance from the Grounds and also from the public road. At the northern end is a productive Fruit Orchard.

The Imposing Range of Span-roof Glass Houses

is divided into seven compartments, the central section forming a Handsome Conservatory with a Rockery at the end, while there are also Two Peach Houses, a Cherry House and Three other Green Houses.

At the rear is a

Brick and Slated Range of Buildings

Including Mushroom House, Fitted Fruit Room, Potting Shed, Boiler House with Drying Room over, Seed Room, Barrow Shed, Carpenter's Shed and Mens's Urinal. Adjoining is a Frame Yard. At a short distance to the South is another commodious Green House. In enclosure No. 6° is a commodious flint and brick Keeper's Cottage with tiled roof, containing kitchen, sitting room, wash house and three bed rooms. At the side is a timber and tiled Store Shed. On the opposite side of the road is a timber and slate Dog Kennel with yards. The Mansion, Grounds, Gardens and Plantations together extend over an area of about

54 a.   2 r.   7 p.

as shown in the following Schedule.

No. on Plan	Description.	Quantity.		
	PARISH OF WOODMANSTERNE.	A.	R.	P.
6a	Plantation	9	2	27
6e	Carriage Drive	2	3	10
6h	North Lodge and Plantation	12	1	17
6l	Plantation	0	2	1
6m	Ditto, etc.	2	0	11
6n	Mansion & Pleasure Grounds, etc.	19	0	6
6o	Keeper's Cottage and Plantation	0	2	12
6p	Rough Pasture and Trees	3	0	23
6r	Three Clumps of Trees	0	0	23
6s	Tennis Court and Ditto	0	2	7
6t	Four Clumps of Trees	0	1	8

cont.

66	Kitchen Garden	1	3	18
68a	Plantation	0	3	4
69a	Ditto	0	1	37
69b	Clump of Trees	0	0	10
	PARISH OF CARSHALTON			
43	—— ——	0	0	33
	Total A.	**54**	**2**	**7**

The foregoing are at present in hand and possession can be given on completion of the purchase.

The Shooting over the Estate is let temporarily, but possession of this also may be had upon completion.

The Model Farmery

is situate on the South Western side of the property and conveniently adjacent to the public road. It is entered through a Covered Porch and includes a brick and flint

Farm House

with tiled roof, containing Two Sitting-Rooms, Kitchen, Scullery, Dairy, Milk Shed and Three Bed Rooms.

The Farm Buildings

are at the rear of the House, and are conveniently arranged on three sides of a Fold Yard. They consist of Store Shed, Cow Shed for seven; Mixing Shed and Boiler House; Root and Hay Stores; a range of Three Piggeries with yards; Cattle Box and Calf Pen; three-arch open Cattle Shed; Calf House with Chaff Loft over; Four-bay open Cattle Shed with enclosed Box at end. At the rear is an Engine House with Boiler and Oil Engine fitted for driving the Farm machinery, and a Saw Bench.

Another range includes Tool Shed; Four-bay Wagon Shed with Granary over; Four-stalled Stable with a Fodder Store; a timber and slated range consisting of Implement Sheds; Barn; Three-division Bullock Shed with Lambing Yard adjoining. There are also a detached Fowl House, Lambing Shed and Aviary.

In the enclosure, shown as No.6b on Sale Plan, is a brick and corrugated iron Lambing Shed.

The foregoing, together with the healthy Park Land and enclosures under arable cultivation, embrace an area of about

125 a.   3 r.   14 p.

as shewn in the following Schedule:-

No. on Plan.	Description.	Cultivation.	Quantity		
	PARISH OF WOODMANSTERNE.		A.	R.	P.
6b	The Forty-four Acres	Arable	44	1	3
6c	Stack Yard	—	0	1	14
6d	Part of The Park	Pasture	7	1	37
6f	Ditto	Ditto	11	0	17
6g	Ditto	Ditto	9	1	4
6i	Ditto	Arable	8	2	15
6q	Ditto	Pasture	0	2	38
6j	Ditto	Ditto	10	0	14
6k	Ditto	Ditto	7	3	15
62	Small Paddock	Ditto	1	1	25
63	The Two Acres	Ditto	2	0	14
Pt. 65	Farmstead, Cottage, etc.	—	0	3	38
68	The Home Field	Pasture	2	2	23
69	Opposite Lodge	Ditto	18	3	37
		Total A	125	3	14

The foregoing are let to Messrs. William George Woodin and William Woodin, under yearly Michaelmas tenancy at a Rental, inclusive of the sum of 17s. 2d. representing interest on capital outlays made by the landlord, of

£125 17s. 2d. per annum

Adjacent to the Farmstead and part of 65 on the Plan is

A Flint and Brick Cottage

Containing Sitting Room, Kitchen and Scullery, together with Three Bed Rooms.
There is a detached timber and tiled Store Shed and a Small Garden.
The foregoing is let to Mr. Beadel under weekly tenancy at a Rental of 7s. 6d. per week, this representing

£19 10s. 0d. per annum

the landlord discharging all rates.

In No. 64 on Sale Plan is a
One-storeyed Brick and Flint Cottage

Containing 4 Rooms, with Shed at the back and productive Garden. On the other
side of the road, and shewn as 66b on the Plan, is a Blacksmith's Shop and
Shoeing-place, the whole embracing an area of about

0a.   1r.   38p.

The foregoing is let to Mr. Harbour under yearly tenancy, at a rental of
£16 per annum

General Summary:-

DESCRIPTION.	OCCUPIER..	QUANTITY.		
		A.	R.	P.
Mansion, Grounds, Stabling, etc.	In hand . .	54	2	7
The Oaks Farm. . . .	Messrs. Woodin	125	3	14
Cottage and Garden . . .	Mr. Beadel .	included above		
Cottage and Smithy . . .	Mr. Harbour .	0	1	38
	Total A.	180	3	19

The property is believed to be free from the payment of Land Tax, but is subject to
Tithe Rent charge, the amount payable for the past year being £27 12s. 2d. and to
Undeveloped Land Duty amounting to £21 3s. 3d. per annum.

The Landlord also pays a sum of £30 per annum to the Sutton District Water
Company in respect of the water supplied to the Mansion, Farm and other
properties on the Estate.

APPENDIX II

YARDAGES FOR THE PROPOSED PRE-SECOND WORLD WAR GOLF COURSE IN THE OAKS PARK:-

Hole 1	-	380 yards
Hole 2	-	150 yards
Hole 3	-	360 yards
Hole 4	-	110 yards
Hole 5	-	360 yards
Hole 6	-	400 yards
Hole 7	-	135 yards
Hole 8	-	470 yards (with large bunkering)
Hole 9	-	340 yards
Hole 10	-	150 yards
Hole 11	-	430 yards
Hole 12	-	190 yards
Hole 13	-	340 yards
Hole 14	-	210 yards (downhill)
Hole 15	-	320 yards (dog-leg)
Hole 16	-	250 yards
Hole 17	-	390 yards
Hole 18	-	480 yards
Total yardage	-	5,465 yards

The above information has been extracted from a copy of a report to Carshalton Urban District Council by Messrs. Dawson and Partners on the lay-out of The Oaks and its estates, October, 1935.

REFERENCES

1   *Surrey Archaeological Collections*, Volume 75, p. 227. "Three later Neolithic discoidal knives from north-east Surrey: with a note on similar examples from the county", by J. Cotton.

2   *Surrey Archaeological Collections*, Volume 66, p. 116. Extracts from the Bulletins of 1968. December . Operation Pipeline again, by E. A. Baxter.

3   *The Past - our Future*, edited by Clive Orton (Beddington Carshalton and Wallington Archaeological Society occasional paper 4, 1980) pp. 8-12: "Settlement patterns in the area around Beddington, Carshalton and Wallington: an outline of archaeological evidence", by Lesley Adkins.

4   *Surrey Archaeological Collections*, Volume 76, pp. 11-50. "New research on a late Bronze Age enclosure at Queen Mary's Hospital, Carshalton", by Lesley Adkins and Stuart Needham.

5   Jones, A.E. *An Illustrated Directory of Old Carshalton*. Published by the author, Carshalton, 1973.

6   *The Archaeology of the London Borough of Sutton: an interim survey*, by Lesley Adkins, for the South-West London Archaeological Unit, March, 1979. Copy in Central Library, Sutton.

7   *Surrey Archaeological Collections*, Volume 69, pp. 37-45. "Woodcote, or Woodcote Warren, once a City according to Tradition", by K.W. Muckleroy.

8   Manning, Reverend Owen , and Bray, William. *The History and Antiquities of the County of Surrey*. 3 vols. 1804-14; Fascimile edition, EP Publishing and Surrey County Library, 1974.

9   *Surrey Archaeological Collections*, Volume 16, pp. 1-27. "Notes on the manor and parish of Woodmansternc", by F.A.H. Lambert. (This volume includes the Lambert family tree.)

10   *The Victoria History of the Counties of England: Surrey*. Published for the University of London Institute of Historical Research. Reprinted from the original edition of 1912 by Dawsons of Pall Mall, London, 1967.

11   Busfield, D.W. *A History of the Surrey Village of Woodmansterne*. First published by the author in April, 1987. Revised and reprinted in May, 1987. Part One to 1900 revised and reprinted December 1990

12   Powick, Sir Maurice. *The Thirteenth Century*, 1216-1307. Oxford History of England. 2nd edition. Oxford University Press, 1962.

13   Brayley, Edward W. *A Topographical History of Surrey*. Revised edition by Edward Walford. 4 vols. Virtue [1878].

14   Lambert, F.A.H. *Surrey*. Methuen & Co., London, 1903.

15   Report of an inspection of the outbuildings at the Oaks Park by Douglas Cluett, 1981. Central Library, Sutton.

16   *Surrey Archaeological Collections*. Volume 14. p.x "Report of the Annual Excursion of the Surrey Archaeological Society held on Wednesday, 28th July, 1893".

17   Dent, John. *The Quest for Nonsuch*. First published April, 1962 by Hutchinson & Co. (Publishers) Ltd. Second edition (revised) August 1970. 1st paperback edition (reprinted from 2nd edition) November, 1981. Reprinted 1988, London Borough of Sutton Leisure Services.

18   Michell, Ronald. *The Carews of Beddington*. London Borough of Sutton Libraries and Arts Services, 1981.

19   Notes by Mrs. J. Carew Richardson from Volume IV, Letters and Papers, Foreign and Domestic, Henry VIII. Notes in Central Library, Sutton.

20   *Surrey Archaeological Collections*. Volume 77, pp. 181-186. "Queen Elizabeth I and the Croydon horse race, with a check list of the Queen's visits to Croydon", by Marion Calthorpe.

21   Smith, R.P. *The History of Sutton A.D. 675-1960: with a Tribute to Carshalton and Banstead Downs*. Derek W. James, Sutton, 1970.

22   Mortimer, Roger. *The History of the Derby Stakes*. Second edition. Michael Joseph Ltd., London, 1973.

23   Mortimer, Roger, with Neligan, Tim. *The Epsom Derby*. Michael Joseph, London, 1984.

24   Jones, Michael Wynn. *The Derby: a Celebration of the World's Most Famous Race*. Croom Helm, London, 1979.

25   Fine annexed to Indenture dated 1st April, 1783. Central Library, Sutton. Sutton Archives, ref: 2/1.

26   Sedgwick, Romney. *The History of Parliament: the Commons 1715-1754.* Volume II E-Y. HMSO 1970.

27   Jones, A.E. *From Medieval Manor to London Suburb: An Obituary of Carshalton.* Published by the author, 1970.

28   Copy will of Sir William Scawen. Surrey Record Office, Kingston-upon-Thames.

29   Parker, Eric. *Highways and Byways in Surrey.* Second edition. Macmillan & Co., Ltd., London, 1950.

30   Toland, John. *The Description of Epsom,* 1711. First published in 1711, now reprinted in facsimile with an introduction by L.C. Silverthorne. Derek W. James, Sutton, Surrey. 1978.

31   Rowan, Alistair. *Lord Derby's Reconstruction of The Oaks.* Burlington Magazine, Vol. 127, pp. 679-687. (October 1985).

32   *Dictionary of National Biography.* Smith, Eldon & Co., London, 1908.

33   Bagley, J.J. *The Earls of Derby, 1485-1985.* Sidgwick & Jackson, London, 1985.

34   Namier, Sir Lewis, and Brooke, John. *The History of Parliament: the House of Commons 1754-1790.* 3 vols. HMSO, 1964.

35   Barrett, CR.B. *Surrey: Highways, Byways and Waterways.* Bliss & Co., London, 1895.

36   Cox, Millard. *Derby: the Life and Times of the Twelfth Earl of Derby, Edward Smith Stanley (1752-1834).* J.A.Allen, London, 1974.

37   Bawtree, Harold. *A Few Notes on Banstead Downs with some remarks on the Epsom races in Olden Times, and a Short Description of Nonsuch Palace and its Surroundings, and of Old Roads in Britain.* William Pile Ltd. , Sutton, 1930. Central Library , Sutton.

38   *Two Hundred and Fifty Years of Map-making in the County of Surrey: a collection of reproductions of printed maps published between the years 1579-1823* with introductory notes by William Ravenhill; Harry Margary, Lympne Castle, Kent, 1974, contains Map of the County of Surrey from an Actual Survey made in the years 1822 and 1823 by C. & I. Greenwood, London. Central Library, Sutton.

39   Thorne, James, *F.S.A. Handbook to the Environs of London, alphabetically arranged, containing an account of every town and village, and of all places of interest, within a circle of twenty miles round London.* J. Murray, London, 1876.

40   Middlekauff, Robert. *The Glorious Cause: the American Revolution 1763-1789.* The Oxford History of the United States, Vol. II. Oxford University Press, New York, London, 1982.

41   Alden, John R. *A History of the American Revolution: Britain and the Loss of the Thirteen Colonies.* Macdonald, London, 1969.

42   Bolton, A.T. *The Architecture of Robert and James Adam, 1758-1794.* 2 volumes. London, Country Life, etc., New York, G. Scribner's Sons, 1922. Volume II - 10, Hertford Street for John Burgoyne (see Index). Volume II - Derby House, Chapter 19 and note 5 to Chapter 19.

43   Binney, Marcus. *Sir Robert Taylor: From Rococo to Neo-Classicism.* London, 1984.

44   Bolton, A.T. *The Architecture of Robert and James Adam, 1758-1794.* 2 volumes. London, Country Life, etc., New York, G. Scribner's sons, 1922. Volume II Chapter XIX, and notes 3, 7, 9, 10. Volume II Chapter XX. The Oaks Pavilion, and notes 2, 3, 7.

45   Extract from *The Gentleman's Magazine,* June, 1774. Central Library, Sutton.

46   *The London Stage: a collection of the most reputed Tragedies, Comedies, Operas, Melo-dramas, Farces and Interludes.* Accurately printed from acting copies, as performed at the Theatre Royal, and carefully collated and revised. Vol. III. London: Published for the Proprietors by Sherwood & Co., Paternoster Row. Copy in Central Library, Sutton.

47   Copy of Indenture of Lease, 6th February, 1775. (From original at Knowsley) Central Library, Sutton.

48   Bolton, *A.T. The Architecture of Robert and James Adam, 1758-1794.* 2 volumes. London, Country Life, etc., New York, G. Scribner's Sons, 1922. Volume II, Chapter XIX and note 5.

49   *Coulsdon Downland Village,* edited by Una Broadbent and Ronald Latham. Published by the Bourne Society, 1976.

50   Tharby, *W.G. The History of Coulsdon West.* Published by the Coulsdon West Residents' Association, 1972.

51   *Surrey County Magazine,* May/June 1977.

52   Seth-Smith, Michael, and Mortimer, Roger. *Derby 200: the Official Story of the Blue Riband of the Turf.* Guinness Superlatives Ltd. , Enfield, Middx., 1979.

53   Hassell, John. Picturesque *Rides and Walks, with excursions by water, thirty miles round the British Metropolis.* Volume 1, 1817. 2 vols. F.P., London, 1817-18. British Library. Microfilmed extract in Central Library, Sutton.

54   *Encyclopaedia Britannica.* Encyclopaedia Britannica Limited, London, 1962.

55   *Harmsworth's Universal Encyclopedia,* edited by J.A. Hammerton. 9 vols. The Amalgamated Press Ltd., London, 1920.

56   Bolton, A.T. *The Architecture of Robert and James Adam,* 1758-1794. 2 volumes. London, Country Life, etc., New York, G. Scribner's Sons, 1922. Chapter XX. Note 7.

57   Fleming, Laurence, and Gore, Alan. The English Garden. Appendix 2. p. 243. Michael Joseph Ltd., London, 1979.

58   Letter from Mr. A. Maynard-Taylor to Mr. Douglas Cluett, 2nd June, 1977. Central Library, Sutton.

59   Bolton, A.T. *The Architecture of Robert and James Adam,* 1758-1794. 2 volumes. London, Country Life, etc., New York, G. Scribner's Sons, 1922. Chapter XIX. Note 5b.

60   *Surrey Archaeological Collections,* Volume 43, pp. 1-15 (p. 13). "Hunting in Surrey", by the Earl of Onslow, P.C. , F.S.A.

61   Plan with brochure of The Oaks. Mrs. James's Sale, 1912. Central Library, Sutton.

62   Cunningham, M. *The Story of Little Woodcote and Woodcote Hall.* Heritage in Sutton Leisure, 1989.

63   Brightling, George B. *Some Particulars Relating to the History and Antiquities of Carshalton.* 1st edition 1872, 2nd edition 1882. Facsimile reprint of 2nd edition with added index, London Borough of Sutton Libraries and Arts Services, 1978.

64   Ordnance Survey map, 2nd edition, twenty-five inches to the mile. 1896. Central Library, Sutton.

65   Woodmansterne Parish Registers. Micro-fiche copies, Central Library, Sutton.

66   Carshalton Urban District Council Guide, 1963. Central Library, Sutton.

67   Beasley, Maureen. *Five Centuries of Artists in Sutton: a Biographical Dictionary of Artists Associated with Sutton, London.* Sutton Libraries and Arts Services, 1989.

68   Greville, Charles. *The Greville Diary.* 2 vols. Vol. I. Edited by Philip Whitwell Wilson. London, W. Heinemann, 1927.

69   Greville, Charles. *The Greville Memoirs, 1814-1816.* 7 vols. Vol. II. Edited by Lyttton Strachey and Roger Fulford. London, Macmillan & Co., 1938.

70   Copy of Indenture of Sale. 4th February, 1834. Central Library, Sutton. Original held by Legal Section, London Borough of Sutton Chief Executive's Office.

71   *Burke's Peerage,* 1879.

72   Greville, Charles. *The Greville Memoirs, 1814-1860.* 7 vols. Vol. III. Edited by Lytton Strachey and Roger Fulford. London, Macmillan & Co., 1938.

73   Greville, Charles. *The Greville Memoirs, 1814-1860.* 7 vols. Vol. V. Edited by Lytton Strachey and Roger Fulford. London, Macmillan & Co., 1938.

74   Copy of Conveyance, 25th December, 1842. Central Library, Sutton. Original held by Legal Section, London Borough of Sutton Chief Executive's Office.

75   Tupper, Martin Farquhar. *Surrey: a rapid review of its principal interests, in persons and places; also St. Martha's, a poem; and a geological sketch of the county.* Guildford, E. Andrews, 1849.

76   Schedule of Deeds and documents relating to The Oaks and the Oaks Farm. Central Library, Sutton. Originals held by Legal Section, London Borough of Sutton Chief Executive's Office.

77   Copy of an extract from the sale catalogue, 1873. Central Library, Sutton.

78   Copy will of Daniel Aldersley Taylor. Surrey Record Office, Kingston upon Thames.

79   Copy of letter from Mr. A. Maynard-Taylor to Mr. Douglas Cluett, 14th December, 1977. Central Library, Sutton.

80 Extract from the *Surrey County Journal,* April/June, 1958, from an article on Heath House, Banstead, and The Oaks. Central Library, Sutton.

81 Copy of letter from Mr. A. Maynard-Taylor to Mr. Douglas Cluett, 26th April, 1981. Central Library, Sutton.

82 Indenture of re-conveyance of mortgage, 9th November, 1888; in schedule of Deeds and documents relating to The Oaks and the Oaks Farm. Central Library, Sutton. Originals held by Legal Section, London Borough of Sutton Chief Executive's Office.

83 Information from the Woodmansterne Parish Registers supplied by the Reverend C.C. Cooper, T.D., A.K.C., Rector of St. Peter's Church, Woodmansterne.

84 Sales brochure of The Oaks, July 1912. Central Library, Sutton.

85 Copy of Indenture dated 3rd May, 1915. Central Library, Sutton.

86 Lambert, Sir Henry. *Woodmansterne: a Brief Historical Account.* Sutton, W. Pile, [1931]

87 The late Mrs. H. Herbecq's memories of The Oaks when open to the public by Carshalton Urban District Council c.1935. Given verbally to author.

88 Surrey County Council documents relating to The Oaks. Ref: CC 86. Surrey Record Office, County Hall, Kingston-upon-Thames.

89 Copy of a report to Carshalton Urban District Council by Messrs. Dawson and Partners on the lay-out of The Oaks and its estate, October, 1935. Central Library, Sutton.

90 Details of the proposed golf course at The Oaks from report. Central Library, Sutton.

91 Copy of a letter from Mr. David Lewry to Lord Crook of Carshalton. Central Library, Sutton

92 Article in the *Wallington and Carshalton Herald Extra,* week-ending 1st June, 1989.

93 Article in the *Sutton Times* for week-ending 8th February, 1940. Copy in Central Library, Sutton.

94 Petition of the Urban District Council of Carshalton in the County of Surrey for the grant of a Charter of Incorporation as a Municipal Borough. July, 1953. Copy in the possession of Mr. L. Sandell.

95   Article in the *Sutton and Wallington Informer* for week-ending 9th June, 1989.

96   Author's post-war memories of The Oaks and Oaks Park.

97   Carshalton Urban District Council. Agenda and Reports of Committees to be submitted to Council on Wednesday, 23rd March, 1955. Report of General Purposes Committee's meeting on 23rd February, 1955, Appendix "A", report of The Oaks Sub-Committee's meeting on 2nd February, 1955, p. 552-p. 553.

98   Carshalton Urban District Council. Agenda and Reports of Committees to be submitted to the Council on Wednesday, 29th June, 1955. Report of the General Purposes Committee's meetings on 27th April and 1st June, 1955. p. 22-p.24.

99   Carshalton Urban District Council. Agenda and Reports of Committees to be submitted to the Council on Wednesday 25th July, 1956. Report of the General Purposes Committee's meeting on 4th June, 1956. Apppendix "A", report of The Oaks Sub-Committee's meeting on 4th June, 1956, p.101-p.104.

100   Carshalton Urban District Council. Agenda and reports of Committees to be submitted to Council on Wednesday 26th September, 1956. Report of the General Purposes Committee's meeting on 25th July, 1956, p.158.

101   Carshalton Urban District Council. Agenda and Report of Committees to be submitted to Council on Wednesday, 24th October, 1956. Report of the General Purposes Committee's meeting on 26th September, 1956, p.220.

102   Carshalton Urban District Council. Agenda and Reports of Committees to be submitted to Council on Wednesday, 28th November, 1956. Report of the General Purposes Committee's meeting on 24th October, 1956, p.262.

103   Carshalton Urban District Council. Agenda and reports of Committtees to be submitted to Council on Wednesday, 2nd January, 1957. Report of the General Purposes Committee's meeting on 28th November, 1956, Appendix "A", report of The Oaks Sub-Committee's meeting on 12th November, 1956, p.323-p.324.

104   Carshalton Urban District Council. Agenda and Reports of Committees to be submitted to Council on Wednesday, 24th April, 1957. Report of the General Purposes Committee's meeting on 27th March, 1957, p. 537, and Appendix "A", report of a Special Meeting of The Oaks Sub-Committee on 9th March, 1957, p.541-p.542.

105   Extract from the Surrey County Journal, January/March, 1958. Central Library, Sutton.

106   Carshalton Urban District Council. Agenda and Reports of Committees to be submitted to Council on Wednesday, 23rd October, 1957. Report of General Purposes Committee's meeting on 25th September, 1957, Appendix "A", report of The Oaks Sub-Committee's meeting on 27th July, 1957, p.215-p.216.

107   Carshalton Urban District Council. Agenda and Reports of Committees to be submitted to Council on Wednesday, 26th November, 1958, Report of the General Purposes Committee's meeting on 22nd October, 1958, Appendix "A", report of The Oaks Sub-Committee's meeting on 1st October, 1958, p.262-p.263.

108   Carshalton Urban District Council. Agenda and Reports of Committees to be submitted to Council on Wednesday, 1st January, 1959. Report of the General Purposes Committee's meeting on 26th November, 1958, p.319.

109   Carshalton Urban District Council. Agenda and Reports of Committees to be submitted to Council on Wednesday, 28th January, 1959. Report of the General Purposes Committee's meeting on 1st January, 1959, p.372.

110   Carshalton Urban District Council. Agenda and Reports of Committees to be submitted to Council on Wednesday, 25th February, 1959. Report of the General Purposes Committee's meeting on 29th January, 1959, p.413.

111   Carshalton Urban District Council. Agenda and Reports of Committees to be submitted to Council on Wednesday 25th March, 1959. Report of the General Purposes Committee's meeting on 25th February, 1959, p.473.

112   Carshalton Urban District Council. Agenda and Reports of Committees to be submitted to Council on Wednesday. 22nd April, 1959. Report of the General Purposes Committee's meeting on 25th March, 1959 p.527.

113   Carshalton Urban District Council. Agenda and Reports of Committees to be submitted to Council on Wednesday, 1st July, 1959. Report of the General Purposes Committee's meetings on 22nd April and 27th May 1959, p.20.

114   Carshalton Urban District Council. Agenda and Reports of Committees to be submitted to Council on Wednesday, 25th November, 1959. Report of the General Purposes Committee's meeting on 21st October, 1959, p.274.

115   Carshalton Urban District Council. Agenda and Reports of Committees to be submitted to Council on Wednesday, 27th January, 1960. Report of the General Purposes Committee's meeting on 23rd December, 1959, p.363-p.364.

116   Information supplied by Miss H.M. Cant to the author.

117 Local Studies Collection of illustrations of The Oaks, Central Library, Sutton.

118 Article in the *Wallington and Carshalton Herald Extra,* week-ending 1st June , 1989.

119 Information supplied to the author by Mr. G. Horley and Mr. E.F. Bennett of Alphagreen Limited.

120 Extract from the *Sutton and Cheam Herald,* 5th July, 1973.

121 Information supplied by Professor Michael Wilks to the author.

122 Extract from *The Wallington and Carshalton Advertiser,* 12th November, 1981. Central Library, Sutton.

123 Extract from *The Wallington and Carshalton Times,* 21st January, 1982. Central Library, Sutton.

124 Information supplied by, and correspondence in the possession of, Mr. Gordon Rookledge, Chairman of the Carshalton Society.

125 Information supplied to the author by Mrs. Angela Vaughan of the Sutton Conservation Group.

126 Author's memories of the damage caused by the hurricane on 16th October, 1987.

127 Davison, Mark, and Currie, Ian. *Surrey in the Hurricane: October 16, 1987.* Froglets Publications Limited, Brasted, Kent. 1988.

128 Article in *The Sutton & Wallington Informer* week-ending 9th June, 1989.

129 Brochure for the Chasse aux Trésor 1991 published by the Clarkson Hyde Charity Committee.

---

the end.

Adam, James 32
Adam, Robert iii, 10, 16, 17, 19-21, 22, 24, 27, 29, 32, 33, 55, 65, 68, 71, 73, 76, 78
Aldersley, William 57
Alphagreen Ltd., *Messrs* 82
Althorp, *Lord* 51
American War of Independence 34, 35, 36, 37, 38
Anne of Denmark, *Queen Consort of James I* 6
Annual Register 1774, 26
Anson, *family* 48
Antiquities of Surrey by Nathaniel Salmon, 1736 1
Antoninus *(Roman Author)* 2
Archaeology of Oaks site and area 1, 2, 47
Argyll, *Duchess of* 20, 25, 26, 31, 35
Arnull, Sam 39
Aubrey, John 2
Azor *(Saxon Lord)* 2

Backworth, Northumberland 53
Baker, *Rev* William 59
Baldwin, *Lord of le Sap* 2
Bandon 4
Bank of England 8,10,17
Banstead 4, 5, 57, 59, 61
Banstead Downs 5, 6, 8, 9, 48, 80, Col.Plate IV
Banstead Downs Plate 8
Banstead Golf Course 63
Banstead Hospital 48, Col.Plate IV
Banstead Windmill 48, Col.Plate IV
Barenger, James, *junior* 48, Col.Plate IV
Barrow Hedges, *House and Area* 1, 2, 8, 9, 13, 51, Col.Plate III
Barrows *(prehistoric burial mounds)* 1
Barthélemon, François 22,23
Barthélemon, *Mrs* 23
Basque Nationals 66
Beddington (Beddintone) 2, 4, 5, 6
Beddington and Wallington, Borough 82
Beddington, Carshalton and Wallington Archaeological Society 74
Bedford, Duchess of 25, 26
    niece of 20
Bedford, *Duke of* 25
Bentinck, *family* 48
Bentinck, George, *Lord* 51
Betchworth 5

Bienfaite, Richard de (Richard of Tonbridge, Richard Clare) 2, 3
Bligh, *Captain* 48
Blome, Richard 6
'Bloomsbury gang' 25
Bootle-Wilbraham, Edward *(later Lord Skelmersdale)* 49
Bootle-Wilbraham, Emma Caroline 49
Borough, Banstead (Burgh Heath) 9
Boswell, James 40
Boy Scouts 57, 80
Bray, William 47
Brennan, John 87
Bridget, *horse* 39
Brighton 34, 51
Britannia, by William Camden 1
Bromley, Kent 57
Brooks' Club 40
Brown, Lancelot 'Capability' 42
Bunbury, *Sir* Charles 35, 39
Bures, John de 4
Burgess, Henry William 48
Burgh (Heath) 9
Burgoyne, *children* 40, 45
Burgoyne, *Lady* Charlotte *(formerly Lady Charlotte Stanley)* 11, 26, 32
Burgoyne, *Captain* John 11
Burgoyne, *General* John 10-17, 20, 22, 23, 25, 26, 28, 32, 33, 35, 36, 37, 38, 40, 42, 43, 83 **Col.Plate I**
Burgoyne, *Sir* John, *3rd Baronet* 11
Burgoyne, John Fox 40, 43
Burgoyne, Maria Sophie 47
Burke, Edmund 40
Burton, Richard *(17th century author)* 2
Bury St. Edmunds 53
Bute, *Lord* 14

Caldbeck, Kate Morecroft (née Taylor) 57, 59
Caldwall, James 24, 26, 27
Camberwell 55
Cambridge University 17, 43
Camden, William 1
Caravan Club of Great Britain 80, rally **81**
Carew, *Sir* Francis *(d.1611)* 5
Carew, *Sir* Nicholas, K.G. 5
Carew, *Sir* Richard 5
Carlisle, *Countess of* 34
Carlisle, *Lord* 31
Carmallen, *Marquis of* 20
Carshalton 2, 5, 8, 9, 40, 47, 61

Carshalton and Wallington Art Society 87
Carshalton Downs 2
Carshalton House 17
Carshalton on the Hill 80
Carshalton Park (Carshalton Place) 8
Carshalton Society 83, 84
Carshalton Urban District Council 2, 61,
    64, 65, 66, 68, 69, 70, 72, 74, 76, 78,
    80, 82, 86
Caulfield, Susan 40, 43
Charles, *Prince (later* Charles I) 6
Charles II, *King* 6
Charlotte, *Queen Consort of George III*
    iii, 26, 28, 33, 40, 44
Chatham, *Earl of* 14
Cheam 5
Cheam School 45
Chertsey cricket team 33
Chester 59
Chipstead 4
    golf course 63
Civil War (English) 6
Clandon 4
Clare, Gilbert de *(later Earl of Gloucester)*
    3
Clare de, Isabel *(later* Isabel Marshall) 3
Clare, Isabel de (*neé* Marshall) 3
Clare, Richard de (Richard of Tonbridge,
    Richard de Bienfaite) 2, 3
Clarendon, *Earl of* 6
Clarke, Nevisa 61
Clarkson Hyde and Co. 87, 88
Clive ('of India') *Lord* 16
'Club, The' 54
Cocces *or* Cotes, Robert 4
Cocharde, Henry *and* Robert de la 4
Cock-fighting 8, 13, 17, 33, 39, 40, 42,
    43, 52, 57
Cole, *Lady* Elizabeth 44
Cole, Stephen 44
Constable, John 48
Coomber, Malcolm 87
Cotes, John 4
    Robert 4
Coulsdon 4, 33, 34
    Cricket Club 33
    Lion Green 33
Coventry 54
Coventry, *Lady, (née* Maria Gunning)
    20
Cowleshaw, H 80
Cranfield Road West 80
Cricket matches at the Oaks 33, 34,
    Col.Plate II
Croydon 5, 6, 29
Croydon Aviation Research Group 87

Croydon Lane 1, 56, 80, 86, 88
Cuddington 5
Culzean Castle, Ayrshire 32
Cumberland, Richard 43

Dalston Hall, Westmoreland 44
Damer, *Mrs.* 40
Dawson & Partners, *Messrs.* 64
Day, John 82
de la Cocharde, Henry *and* Robert 4
de St. Alban, Adam 4
    John 4
Declaration of Independence, American
    33
Delaney, Mary 22, 23, 25, 26
Demolition and Construction Company
    Ltd 76
Derby, *Earls of, see* Stanley
Derby, The. *Horse-race* iii, 39, 40, 43, 47,
    48, 49, 51, 57, 84
Derby Chapel, Ormskirk 32
Derby House, Grosvenor Square 17, 19,
    26, 29, 32, 33, 35
'Devil's Mounds' *(prehistoric burial
    mounds)* 1
Devonshire, *Duke of* 13, 20
Devonshire, Georgiana, *Duchess of* 34
Diomed, *horse* 39
Domesday Survey 2, 3
Dorset, *Duke of* 20, 33, 34, 35
Downlands iii, 4, 5, 6, 8, 9, 10, 17, 34, 39,
    40, 47, 66, **Col.Plate IV**
Drury Lane Theatre 19, 28, 43
Durand, John *(d. 1788).* 47
Durand, John Hodsdon 39, 40, 47

East India Company 16
Ebbutt, John 29
Edwin, *Lady* Charlotte 26
Effingham 64
Egerton, *Thomas, 2nd Earl of Wilton* 45
Eglington, *Countess of* 34
Elizabeth, *Queen* 6
Elliott, *Lt. Col.* 14
Environment, Department of 83
Epsom 5, 6, 9
    Spa 6, 9, 29
Epsom Downs iii, 5, 6, 8, 17, 39, 47, 51
Epsom grandstand 84, 86
Epsom race-course 83, 84
Errol, *Lord and Lady* 51
Essex, *Countess of* 34
Eton College 17, 43, 48
Evelyn, John 2
Ever Ready Ltd. 83, 84
Ewell 5
Excellent, H.M.S. 48

Farren, Elizabeth (Eliza)(*later Countess of Derby*) 42-45, **46**, 49, 51, 52
Farren, George 42
Fête Champêtre, 1774 iii, 20, 21, 22, 23, **24**, 25, 26, **27**, 28, 29, 34, 47, 83
Fitzroy, *Lord* Charles 53
Forester, Reginald le 4
Forrester, *family* 48
Fort William 16
Fox, Charles 31, 37, 40, 43
Fuller, Moon & Fuller, *Messrs* 61

Gallop, The. *road* 2
'Gally Hills' *(prehistoric burial mounds)* 1
Garratts Hall, Banstead 4, 59
Garrick, David 28
Gas pipe, London ring-main, laying 1, 2
Gatton 4
Gentleman's Magazine, June 1774 26
George III, *King* iii, 26, 28, 32, 33, 35
George IV, *King (formerly Prince Regent, formerly Prince of Wales)* iii, 26, 40, 45, 48
George of Denmark, *Prince Consort to Queen Anne* 8
Gilby Racing 84
Gilliat, Augusta *(later* Smith) 54
Gilpin, *Rev.* William, senior 45
Gipps, *Sir* George 53
Girl Guides 57, 80
Glenelg, *Lord* 54
Gloucester, Honour of, The 3
Goebbels, Paul Joseph 66
Golf Course(s) 1, 63, 64, 65, 67, 80, 82, 83, 86, 87, 88
Gosford, *Lord* 53
Gosling, *Sir* Thomas 10, 17
Gower, *Dowager Countess of* 25, 26
Grafton, *Duke of* 34, 51, 53
Grafton Street 17
Graham, *Mr.* 51
Green Belt 65
Greenacres School for Girls 57, 58
Grenville, George 14
Greville, Charles 49, 51, 53, 54
Grey, *Earl* 51
Grey, *Sir* Charles Edward 51, 53, 54
Grey, Elizabeth, *Lady (née* Jervoise) 54
Grey, *Lt.Col.* John 51
Grey, R.W. 53
Greyhound Inn, Carshalton 8, 40, 47
Griffiths Ltd., *Messrs* Charles 78
Grignion, C 24, 26, 27
Grosvenor Square 17, 26, 29, 31, 32, 33, 35, 45
'Grotto' (conservatory) 56, 66, 80, 86, 88

Guilton, Kent 42
Gunning, Elizabeth, *(Later Duchess of Hamilton, later Countess of Argyll)* 20, 25, 26, 31, 35
Gunning, Maria, *(Later Lady Coventry)* 20
Hamilton, *Lord* Archibald, *(later 7th Duke of)* 26, 40
Hamilton, E.C. 84
Hamilton, *Lady* Elizabeth (Betty) *(later Countess of Derby)* iii, 20, 23, 25, 26, 29, **30**, 31, 33, 34, 35, **Col.Plate II**
Hamilton, Elizabeth, *Duchess of (later Countess of Argyll)* 20
Hamilton, James, *6th Duke of* 20
Hassell, John 49
'Haw-Haw, Lord' (William Joyce) 66
Hawking 6
Haymarket Theatre 42, 43
Hazlitt, William 43
Heath House, Banstead 57
Henry VIII, *King* 5
Henry, *Prince, son of James I* 6
Hermione, *horse* 40, 43
Hertford Street, Mayfair 16
Higgins, Richard 59
Higher Baldington, Cheshire 57
Historic Buildings and Ancient Monuments Act, 1953 72
Historic Buildings Bureau 72
Historic Buildings Council for England 72, 74
Hoghton, *Sir* Henry 14, 16
Holyrood Palace, Edinburgh 20
Home Guard 66, 80,
    seat **79**
Horley 4, 47
Hornby, Charlotte (*née* Stanley) 44
Hornby, Charlotte Margaret 45
Hornby, Edmund 44
Hornby, Edward 45
Hornby, *Rev.* Geoffrey 44, 45, 47
Hornby, *Sir* Geoffrey Thomas Phipps 48
Hornby, *Rev.* James John 48
Hornby, *Hon.* Lucy 44, 45, 47
Hornby, Phipps 47, 48
Horndean, Hampshire 53
Horne 4
Horse-racing 5, 6, 8, 9, 13, 17, 20, 33, 39, 40, 45, 47, 48, 49, 51, 57
Housing and Local Government, Ministry of 70, 72, 74, 76, 78
Howe, *Lord* 17
Hunt, Henry 52
Hunters' Club, The 9, 10

Hunting 5, 6, 10, 40, 47, 63
Hurricane and gales, damage from 86,
   87, 88

Isleworth Park 53

James I, *King* 6
James, *6th Duke of Hamilton* 20
James, Adrian Ingham 59
James, Harry Berkeley 59, 61
James, Inez Mary 61
James, Lucy 59, 61, 63, 64
Jervoise, Elizabeth, *Lady* 53
Jervoise, Elizabeth *(later Lady Grey)* 53,
   54
Jervoise, *Rev. Sir* Samuel 53
Jockey Club 13, 20, 29, 39, 40, 51, 83, 84
Johnson, *Dr.* Samuel 40, 54
Jones, Emma 54
Jones, Emma *(née* Smith) 54
Jones, John 54, 55
Jones, John Algernon 54
Jones, Mary 54
Joyce, William 66

Kauffman, Angelica 30
Kelly, *Earl of* 25
Kemble, *Mr. and Mrs.* 40
Kent County cricket team 33
Kew House 26
Knowsley, Lancs 11, 13, 32, 35, 42, 45,
   49, 51
Knowsley Park. Race course 13

Lambert, Ann *(née* Moys) 5
Lambert, Daniel 5
Lambert, Elizabeth 5
Lambert, F.A.H 10, 59
Lambert, George Patrick 48
Lambert, Jeffrey I, *son of John VII* 4
Lambert, Jeffrey II, *(late c17)* 9
Lambert, Jeffrey III, (d.1742), *son of John
   VIII* 10
Lambert, John I, *(c13)* 3, 4
Lambert, John II, *son of John I (alive
   1301, conveys property to son 1333)* 4
Lambert, John III, *son of John II (received
   Lambert's Oaks 1333)* 4
Lambert, John IV *second son of
   Radulphus; ('of Banstead and
   Woodmansterne')* 4
Lambert, John V. *(alive 1432), son of
   John IV* 4
Lambert, John VI, *son of John V* 4
Lambert, John VII, *son of John VI (alive
   1513)* 4 47
Lambert, John VIII *(d. 1721), son of
   Jeffrey II* 9, 10

Lambert, John IX *(d.1771)* 10, 29
Lambert, Mary 48
Lambert, Nicholas, *brother of Roger* 5
Lambert, Nutty 48
Lambert, Radulphus de *(came to England
   with William I)* 2, 3
Lambert, Radulphus, *third son of John III,
   (alive 1377)* 4
Lambert, Roger I *son of Jeffrey I* 4, 5
Lambert, Roger II *(1601-1688) son of
   Daniel and Susan* 5, 9
Lambert, Roger III *(alive in 1668) son of
   Roger II* 9
Lambert, Susan, *(née* Wonham), *wife of
   Daniel* 5
Lambert, William *(b. c.1761)* 10, 29, 42,
   48
Lambert, William, *grandchild of William
   b. c.1761* 48
Lambert, William *(alive 1849)* 55
Lambert's Oaks. *House. see* Oaks, The.
   House.
Lambert's Oaks, The. Public house 10
Lambert's Oaks Down 42
Lauzen, *Duc de* 19
Lawrence, *Sir* Thomas 43, 46, 49
le Forester, Reginald 4
le Lippe, *Count* 14
le Sap, Baldwin, *Lord of* 2
Leatherhead 29
Legrand, Jane 42
Lennox, *Lady* Sarah 35
Lichfield 51
Lindley, Joseph *and* Crosley, William 13
Lion Green *(cricket green)*, Coulsdon 33
Lippe, *Count* le 14
Literary Club, The 54
Little Woodcote 1, 2, 40, 47
Liverpool 57
Lodges 61, 80, 82
London County Council 65
London Gazette 8
'London in Bloom' 86
London ring-main gas pipe laying 1, 2
Lord of the Manor, The 38
Lord's Cricket Ground 34
Lowenstein, Lazares Marcus 64
Lye, Adam a 4

Macphair, *Pilot Officer* 66, 87
Maid of the Oaks, The 22, 23, 25, 28, 29,
   83
Mann, Horace 33
Mann, *Sir* Thomas 22
Manning, *Rev.* Owen 47
Mansion House, City of London 10

March, *Lord* 19, 25, 26
Marshall, Isabel (*later* Clare) 3
Marshall, Isabel (*née* Clare) 3
Marshall, William 3
Mary I, *Queen* 6
Masque: *The Maid of the Oaks* 22, 23, 25, 28, 29, 83
Maynard-Taylor, A. 57
Maynard-Taylor, Daniel. 57, 59
Mears & Son, *Messrs* Ebenezer 74
Medical Research Council's Laboratories 59
Melbourne, *Lord* 54
Mitcham Golf Course 63
Moon, Hilary 82
Morecroft, Louisa, (*later* Taylor) 57, 59
Morecroft, Thomas 57
Moys, Ann, (*later* Lambert) 5
Mure, *Baron* 20, 26
Murray, Charlotte Jane 61
Murray, Inez Mary (*née* James) 61
Murray, John 61
Murray, Malcolm Brown 61

Nash, John 68
National Ancient Monuments Society 68
National Horseracing Museum 83
National Society for the Prevention of Cruelty to Children 87, 88
National Trust 68
Neligan, Tim 84
Nelson, Horatio 48
Nevill, Ralph 59
Newcastle, *Duke of* 14
Newmarket 17, 40
Noiomagus/Noviomagus 2
Nonsuch Palace and Parks 5, 6
North, *Lord* 16, 22, 31, 37
Noviomagus/Noiomagus 2
Nye, David 74

Oakcraft 83, 84
Oakhurst Rise 64, 80
Oaks, The. *Horse-race* iii, 39, 40, 43, 49, 57, 83
Oaks, The. *House*
    passim
    50, 60, 62, 69, 71, 73, 75
    'ale-house' 10
    demolition of iii, 70-78, **77**
    fire and rebuilding 55
    outbuildings 56, 88
    prehistory and archaeology of site 1, 2
Oaks Down 42
Oaks Farm 1, 13, 55, 56, 57, 59, 61, 63, 64
Oaks Park iii, 1, 64, 65, 66, 67, 78, **79**, 80, **81**, 82, **85**, 86, 87, 88

Oaks Park Sports Centre 64, 65, 82, 87
Odermerestor (Saxon Woodcote) 2, 3
Ormskirk 32, 52
Oxford University 49, 53

Palmer, John 43
Parish boundary changes 61
Parsons, Nancy 34
Patten House, Preston, Lancs 13
Pavilion for Fête Champêtre 20-27, **21, 24, 27**
Peel, Robert 51
Pepys, Samuel 6
Perrotts Manor 4
Peter, Thomas 29
Pine Walk, Carshalton 2
Pitt, William, the elder, Earl of Chatham 14
Pocket, Russell 88
Portsmouth 88
Potter, *Mr. (gamecock breeder)* 42
Preston 13, 14, 17, 43, 44, 51, 52, Grammar School 17
Prosser, G.F. 50
Ptolemy 2
Purley Golf Course 63

Queen Mary's Hospital 47
    prehistoric site 1, 2

Radulphus de Lambert 2
Ranelagh Pleasure Gardens 31, 33
Red Lion Inn, Coulsdon 33
Regatta on Thames, Westminster Bridge - London Bridge, 1775 29, 31
Reigate 5
Restaurant and refreshments 80, 82, 87
Reynolds, Sir Joshua Col. Plate 1
Richard de Bienfaite, *or* Richard of Tonbridge, *or* Richard de Clare 2
Richmond, *Duke & Duchess of* 51
Rocque, John 13
Roman remains in area (not Oaks site) 2
Romney, George 41, 49
Rookledge, Gordon 83, 84
Rosebery, *Lord* 39
Royal Academy 48
Royal Fine Art Commission 68
'Rubing' (Rubbing) House, Borrow Hedges 9
Rushton and Co, *Messrs*. John 78

Sackville, John Frederick, (*later Duke of Dorset)* 20, 33, 34, 35
St. Alban, Adam de 4
    John de 4
St. Leger, The. *Horse-race* 49

St. Peter's Church, Woodmansterne 10, 47, 48, 54, 55, 56, 59, 61, 63
St. Raphael's Hospice 88
Salmon, Nathaniel 1
Saltram, *horse* 47
Saratoga, surrender at 37, 38
Saxon remains in area 2
Scawen, *Sir* William 8
Selwyn, George 26, 31, 40
Senex, John 9
Seven Years' War 13, 14
Sheep-farming 4
Sheet Anchor, *horse* 47
Shooting 49, 63
Short, *family*, of Carshalton 8
   Elizabeth; George; Joseph; Peter; Susannah 8
Shortes Place. *House* 4, 5, 9, 48, 59
Shortesland. Estate or sub-manor 4
Simmons, *Mr. Lessee of Lambert's Oaks, early c18* 10
Sir Peter Teazle, *horse* 39, 43
Sir Thomas, *horse* 48
Skelmersdale, *Lord* 49
Smith, Alice 55
Smith, Alice Augusta 55
Smith, Augusta (*née* Gilliat) 54
Smith, Emma, (*later* Jones) 54
Smith, Frederick 54, 55
Smith, Frederick Ernest Gilliat 55
Smith, Frederick Gilliat 55, 57
Smith, Harold Gilliat 55
Smith, Hugh 13
Smith, Jessie Annette 55
Smith, Jessie Lilian Gilliat 55
Smith, Joseph 54, 55, 57, 62
Smith, Lucy, (*later Lady Strange*) 13
Smith, Mabel Rose Gilliat 55
Soane, *Sir* John 68
Society for the Protection of Ancient Buildings 68, 72, 74
South Eastern Gas Board 82
Spanish Civil War 66
Spitfire crash 66, 87
Sports facilities *and* Oaks Park Sports Centre 64, 65, 82, 87
Stag Field 47
Staghounds 45, 47, 49, **Col.Plate IV**
Stamp Act 14, 16
Stanley, Charlotte, *Countess of Derby, wife of 13th Earl* 45
Stanley, *Lady* Charlotte, *daughter of 12th Earl of Derby* 33, 44
Stanley, *Lady* Charlotte, (*later Lady Charlotte, Mrs. Burgoyne*) 11, 26, 32

Stanley, Edward, (*later 11th Earl of Derby*) 11, 13, 17, 29, 32
Stanley, Edward George Geoffrey Smith, (*later 14th Earl of Derby*) 48, 49, 51, 52, **Col.Plate IV**
Stanley, Edward Henry, (*later 15th Earl of Derby*) 49
Stanley, Edward John, *18th Earl of Derby* 84
Stanley, Edward Smith, *Lord Strange, (later 12th Earl of Derby)* iii, 13, 17, 19, 20, 22, 23, 25, 26, 29, **30**, 31, 32, 33, 34, 35, 37, 38, 39-52, **41**, 57, 63, 66, 76, Col.Plate IV
Stanley, Edward Smith, (*later 13th Earl of Derby*) 29, **30**, 43, 45, 47, 48, 49, 61, 63, **Col.Plate IV**
Stanley, Elizabeth (Betty),(*née* Hamilton), *Countess of Derby, 1st wife of 12th Earl* iii, 20, 23, 25, 26, 29,II, **30**, 31, 33, 34, 35, 40, 44, Col.Plate II
Stanley, Elizabeth (Eliza),(*née* Farren), *Countess of Derby, 2nd wife of 12th Earl* 42-45, **46**, 49, 51, 52
Stanley, *Lady* Elizabeth Henrietta (*later* Cole) 36, 44
Stanley, Hans 14
Stanley, James, (*later 10th Earl of Derby*) 11, 13
Stanley, James, (*later* James Smith Stanley, *Lord Strange*) 11, 13, 14, 16, 17
Stanley, James Smith (*son of 12th Earl of Derby*) 45
Stanley, Lady Lucy Elizabeth (*daughter of 12th Earl of Derby*) 45
Stanley, *Lady* Mary Margaret (*later Countess of Wilton*) 45, 49
Stanley Road 80
Stock, Percy 82
Stockbridge 49
Storer, *Miss* 19
Stovie, *Rev.* John George 55
Strange, *Lord* (James Smith Stanley) 11, 13, 14, 16, 17
Stuart, Andrew 26
Surrey Archaeological Society 59
Surrey Battalion Home Guard 66
Surrey County Council 64, 65, 68, 70, 72, 74, 76, 78
Surrey Foxhounds 63
Surrey Joint Poor Law Committee 64
Surrey Staghounds 47, 63
Sutton 5
Sutton, London Borough of 82, 84, 86, 87

Sutton and Cheam, Borough 82
Sutton Arts Council 83
Sutton Conservation Group 86
Sutton Lane 57
Sutton Park, Bedfordshire 11
Sutton District Water Company 56, 63

Taylor, A. Maynard- 57
Taylor, Daniel 57
Taylor, Daniel Aldersley 57, 59
Taylor, Daniel Maynard 57, 59
Taylor, Elizabeth Johnston 57
Taylor, Kate Morecroft 57, 59
Taylor, Louisa (*née* Morecroft) *wife of*
    Daniel Aldersley Taylor 57, 59
Taylor, *Sir* Robert 10, 12, 15, 16, 33, 55,
    65
Taylor, Sophia (*née* Stephens Aldersley)
    57
Taylor, Sophia Louisa 57
Toland, John 8
Tonbridge, Richard of (Richard de
    Bienfaite, Richard de Clare) 2, 3
Town and Country Planning, Ministry of
    68
Town and Country Planning Act, 1947 70
Treasure Hunt 87-88
Trinity College, Cambridge 17
Tunbridge Wells 6, 47
Twickenham 44
Tynemouth 54

Uffenbach, Conrad von 9
United Racecourses Ltd 84
University College, Oxford 53
Upper Ossory, *Countess of* 19, 31
Uxbridge 51

Vauxhall Pleasure Gardens 22
Vernon, *Mr.* 23
Victory, H.M.S 48
Voller, June 83
Von Uffenbach, Conrad 9

Wales, *Prince of, (later Prince Regent,*
    later George IV) iii, 26, 40, 45, 48
Walpole, Horace 19, 22, 31, 33, 40, 42, 43
Walton & Lee, *Messrs.* 61
Walton Heath Golf Course 63
Walton-le-Dale, Lancs. 13
Walton on the Hill 5
War Damage Commission 72
Warren, The. Royal hunting box 6, 9
Weald Hall, Essex 13
Wellys *or* Waleys, Joan, of
    Woodmansterne, (*later* Lambert) 4

West Norwood 59
Westminster Abbey 43
Westminster School 11
White's Club 29
Wilkes, John 37
William IV, *King* 53, 54
Williams, *Sir* William Peere 14
Wilson, L. 74
Winchester 34
Winder, *Rev.* T.E., *Dean of Ossory* 61
Winwick, Lancs. 44
Wonham, Susan, (*later* Lambert) 5
Wonham Manor, Betchworth 5
Woodcote 1, 2, 5
Woodcote, Little 1, 2, 40, 47
Woodcote Hall 47
Woodcote Lodge 40, 47
Woodcote Park Golf Course 63
Woodcote Warren 2
Woodmansterne 1, 2, 3, 4, 5, 29, 30, 42,
    47, 48, 55, 59, 61,
    earlier names 2, 3
Woodmansterne Church (St. Peter's) 10,
    47, 48, 54, 55, 56, 59, 61, 63
Woodmansterne Road 64, 80, 86
Woolwich 43
Works, Ministry of 68, 72, 74
World War II iii, 66, 68, 80, 86
Wrottesley, *Miss* 19
Wroughton, *Mr.* 44

Yates, Gideon Col.Plate III
York, *Duke of* 51
Young, *Sir* G.F 54